The
Compassionate
Organization

And the People Who Love to Work for Them.

ETHAN CHAZIN MBA

authorHOUSE®

AuthorHouse™
1663 Liberty Drive
Bloomington, IN 47403
www.authorhouse.com
Phone: 1 (800) 839-8640

Published by AuthorHouse 11/22/2017

ISBN: 978-1-5462-1707-7 (sc)
ISBN: 978-1-5462-1706-0 (e)

Print information available on the last page.

Any people depicted in stock imagery provided by Thinkstock are models, and such images are being used for illustrative purposes only.
Certain stock imagery © Thinkstock.

This book is printed on acid-free paper.

CONTENTS

Preface

The goal of creating a Compassionate organization should not be short-term financial success. The transformational leaders that build and guide compassionate organizations are not concerned with spewing buzzwords like world-class culture, eco-sustainability or corporate social responsibility for self-promotion.

Compassionate organizations are built upon the 4-P leadership model of caring for your people, the planet, a sense of long-term legacy called your purpose and overall behavioral probity...a powerful moral compass that guides all your decision-making and treatment of others.

Organizations that employ compassion as a central ideology and methodology are able to recruit and keep top talent. They care genuinely about unleashing their people's full potential. As a result, they are able to outperform their competitors at every stage and put themselves in a stronger position to adapt and respond to the constantly changing landscapes in which they operate.

These truly unique individuals who are hard-wired by empathy and caring look constantly to forge the most powerful relationships with the stakeholders they engage including: their employees and clients, in addition to the vendors, suppliers, the media, Regulatory agencies... that they interact and partner with.

Compassion is not a trick or short cut to success. It's certainly not a buzzword to throw around in your marketing and sales efforts. Compassion is a central driving force that ensures your organization is ideally positioned for success (however you define it) not just for today but in the future.

My experiences having worked for 20 years in Corporate America, combined with my work as a management consultant, organizational behavior trainer, executive coach, and motivational speaker giving talks to 15,000 people has formed the basis for this book.

Throughout my career I was downsized, right-sized, re-engineered outsourced, offshored and Reduction-In-Forced many times while working in many types of organization, from global multi-national corporations to small family run businesses, and every type of organizational structure (both for-profit and non-profit) that there is.

I have always been fascinated why organizations choose to treat their employees horribly, or why they treat their employees with civility and respect. What makes organizations trust their employees, why are certain managers abusive, controlling and mean-spirited, and what leads others to be passionate about being a transformational leader who puts their people first and does everything in their power to ensure their workers rise to great heights. What leads certain organizations to behave in unethical manner, while others are driven by a strong set of defining core values, ethics, and a moral compass. It is this fascination with organizational best behaviors that led me to write this book.

Teaching at many colleges and Universities has afforded me with a unique perspective on what matters most to Millennials as they chart a course to career advancement through their academic pursuits. Many of my contemporary Generation Xers do not understand Millennials, nor do the Boomers and Matures whose days of reign of power controlling organizations are fast coming to an end.

I welcome this brave new world of compassionate organizations based on a moral construct and ethical standards of caring for employees, giving back to the communities they engage with, and striving to leave the world a better place than what they have inherited. Organizations that consider their legacy and impact as they ask of themselves "*To what end*" will continue to replace the outdated, 20th Century pyramid shaped command-control entity that discards employees like cheap material and care not what their legacies have been.

Acknowledgements

Such an undertaking would not have been possible without the support of my wife, lifetime partner and best friend, Sonya. She is much more socially astute than me, and would have made an exceptional event planner, if not for pursuing a career path in the law. My daughter Karena gives me hope that her Generation Z peers will assist the Millennials in creating a brave new caring and compassionate organizational work culture. These soon-to-be professionals will be left to determine how best to derive profit while remaining competitive in the industries they compete in, without destroying the morale of their people.

Introduction

The organizational times, they are a changing.

In the past, employees went to work for organizations in an implicit agreement that they would provide their skills for fair pay. If they performed well, they would be rewarded with a modicum of job security and perhaps career advancement. Those days of one employer per career are long gone. In today's "contract" economy, workers change jobs between eight to ten times by the time they reach 35 years old.

The Mature workers and Baby Boomers who first introduced the American workplace to mass layoffs in the 1980s when they were in their 30s and 40s, are now leaving the workplace by the tens of thousands every day.

This mass exodus of the Mature workforce and Baby Boomers coincides with Millennial workers taking over roles of increasing importance within organizations. The sheer number of Millennials now entering the workforce will fill the void being left by Matures and Boomers. Estimates are Millennials will constitute 75-80% of the American workforce by 2020. Meanwhile, organizations have been "flattening out" their management ranks as they cast off layers of middle management in the past few decades.

With this huge transfer in the balance of power from older to younger American workers, Millennials bring with them into the workplace a new set of organizational values, beliefs about work, and a set of ethics and expectations about appropriate organizational behavior. These newly minted professionals witnessed first-hand just how poorly their parents and grandparents were treated by the organizations they had committed to during the great American Recession of 2007-2009. Adding insult to injury came the mortgage foreclosure disaster with millions of Americans being cast out of their homes.

Millennials demand that the organizations they work for (and buy from) share their values, possess a moral compass, and must care for the environment.

Sustainability's explosive growth in recent years has been fueled in large part by Millennials with a strong desire to protect the planet.

Further, Millennials want their ideas to not only be solicited by the organizations they commit to, but also implemented. They want their work to have meaning, and they want to be able to make an IMPACT to the organizations they work for and society as a whole NOW. They do not expect to have to wait years "putting in their time" before they can make a difference. They seek out those organizations that offer them the most meaningful and appealing work-life balance options.

In the past, the implicit "Employer-Employee contract" implied that the worker had to do their job, and keep their family/personal lives completely separate from their work. Now with the blurred boundaries that workers have with work-life balance (WLB) challenges, they are looking for more compassionate organizations that not only accommodates their WLB challenges, but also actively assists them in life challenges such as: child adoption, caring for sick children, providing for elderly/infirm parents, grief counseling, drug/alcohol addiction, buying a home, etc.

And that is where "compassion" enters the organizational equation:

Compassion — from the roots passio (suffering) and com (with) — means to suffer with another. Compassion is an innate part of human response to suffering, which is comprised of a three-part experience of noticing another's pain, feeling with another, and responding in some way.

Thus, the drive for compassion in organizations. You say you don't think there is a place for compassion in organizations? Well, there is an ENTIRE group of researchers who have come to the conclusion that compassion should lie at the heart of organizations. They are part of CompassionLab, whose self-expressed purpose is:

"… a **group of organizational researchers** who strive to create a new vision of organizations as sites for the development and expression of compassion. Our focus is on the expression of compassion in work and in the workplace, including emphasis on roles, routines, practices, relationships, teams, and structures that impact the experience of compassion in organizations. We are part of a **broader community of scholars** who are dedicated to developing a perspective on organizations as sites for human growth and the development of human strengths." [1]

Read on to discover the true power being unleashed in today's compassionate organization.

Ethan, Hoboken, New Jersey

---

[1] www.thecompassionlab.com/about-us

1. Your Career Primer

In my first book, "Bulletproof Your Career in Turbulent Times," I discussed the importance of finding the right organization to work for. Ideal organizations best match your personal beliefs, values, and ethics. In the "Compassionate Organization," I now shift focus to the many aspects of organizational behavior that reflect the best behaviors that are most attractive to employees.

For your career and professional success, let me reiterate a central idea from my first book. It is absolutely CRITICAL that you take a new approach to achieve career happiness and engagement.

Begin by finding your DREAM 18-32 organizations. First, find 3-4 industries that are of particular interest to you. Whether its media and entertainment, sports, fashion, consumer electronics...it doesn't matter. Start with 3 to 4 for simplicity sake and to get going. Once you have identified those 3 to 4 industries, conduct research to find the six to eight organizations in EACH industry that you could envision working for.

By starting with 3 to 4 industries and selecting 6-8 organizations in each... that gets you to 18-32 organizations that you can seriously see yourself working for. This is the ideal size of a potential job search that can be best managed to research and pursue those organizations who share your values and ethics. How do you identify those firms you think you could work at? By exploring their *informal culture*, of course. What's the difference between formal and informal culture?

An organization's **FORMAL culture** is what an organization wants to be known for. It's entirely aspirational and may or may not have any basis in reality. It's the messaging they use for self-promotion in their marketing collateral.

The organization's **INFORMAL culture** is how they act when they think no one is watching them. Imagine you put on your Harry Potter Invisibility Cloak and wandered unseen through their workplace.

How can you find out what an organization's informal culture is like? Conduct informational interviews with current or past employees. Find out from them how do employees interact with one another? How do they treat one another? How do they work in teams...or...do they work in teams? Is It an inclusive, participative culture or a cut throat, everyone for themselves culture? You can also speak to people who served organizations you are interested in as a vendor, supplier, or strategic business partner. Maybe they consulted for those organizations.

For example, the culture of Patagonia feels a LOT different than Goldman Sachs. Disney isn't Oracle. And Harley-Davidson would never be confused with British Petroleum. So, find those 18-32 organizations you could see yourself working at, research as much as you can about them, including: their products and services, employee engagement programs, their position in the industry, industry trends and developments, key competitors, and the problems keeping their senior leadership up at night.

Then...package yourself as a set of solutions to solve specific problems and reach out to the senior most person in the Department/Business Unit you'd like to work in and call them. The ultimate goal is to obtain a face-to-face meeting to present yourself as THE critically needed solutions to the problems they are facing.

As you work your way through your list of ideal potential employers, you can cross off the ones that you have engaged and move on to the next all the while adding to your list as you continue to research potential ideal match employers.

2. Emotional Intelligence

It has been nearly 25 years since Peter Solovay and John D. Mayer first used the term "emotional intelligence" or Emotional Quotient (EQ) to describe a different kind of intelligence that many business leaders believe is essential to achieving success in the workplace. Unlike many other business trends that have come and gone, EQ, an intelligence that involves the ability to monitor one's own and others' feelings and emotions and to use that information to guide one's thinking and actions has retained its relevance.[2]

In his 1995 bestselling book, <u>Emotional Intelligence</u>, Daniel Goleman, the "Godfather of EQ" described emotionally intelligent people as those who perceive emotions, use them in thought, understand their meaning, and manage them better than others. Emotionally intelligent people solve emotional problems with less thought, have highly developed verbal skills, and tend to be more open and agreeable than others (Cicetti, 2013). For Goleman, Mayer, and Solovey, emotional intelligence is a personal characteristic much like initiative, self-confidence, and a drive for results (Mittal and Sindhu, 2012).[3] Two plus decades later, compassionate organizations are placing an ever-increasing emphasis on hiring and training employees using Emotional Intelligence (EI) as a cornerstone skill.

We begin with a working definition of EI:

Emotional intelligence is an absolutely critical skill that people require in order to function well in their personal lives as well as the organizations they work in. It is the field of study in which we delve into people's innate ability to get along with others, and manage their own emotions in the process. EI is the ability to identify and manage your own emotions and the emotions of others. It is generally said to include three key skill sets:

---

[2] Emotional Intelligence: Can Companies Really Feel Their Way to Success? Lauren Garris, Client Relationship Manager, UNC Executive Development.

[3] Emotional Intelligence: Can Companies Really Feel Their Way to Success? Lauren Garris, Client Relationship Manager, UNC Executive Development.

1. Emotional awareness, including the ability to identify your own emotions and those of others;
2. The ability to harness emotions and apply them to tasks like thinking and problems solving; and
3. The ability to manage emotions, including the ability to regulate your own emotions, and the ability to cheer up or calm down another person.[4]

The Power of EI

Studies have found that high emotional intelligence in organizations is associated with increased productivity, higher engagement levels, lower turnover and absenteeism rates, and increased market share. Goleman has theorized that 80 to 90 percent of the competencies that differentiate high-performing workers from average-performing workers can be found in the emotional intelligence domain, and one study (Mount in Freedman, 2010) found emotional intelligence to be two times more predictive of business performance than employee skills, knowledge, and expertise.[5]

We know from research (and common sense) that people who understand and manage their own and others' emotions make better leaders. This is fact, not conjecture. Emotionally intelligent employees are able to deal with stress, overcome obstacles, and inspire others to work toward shared goals. They manage conflict more effectively and build stronger teams. On top of all those benefits of hiring for emotional intelligence, these EI-savvy workers are generally happier at work, too. But far too many managers lack basic self-awareness and social skills.[6]

They don't recognize the impact of their own feelings and moods and tend to struggle to form meaningful workplace relationships. I know…I worked for many such individuals throughout my time spent in Corporate America. They are less adaptable than they need to be in today's fast-paced world. And they don't demonstrate basic empathy for others: they don't understand

---

[4] www.psychologytoday.com/basics/emotional-intelligence.
[5] Emotional Intelligence: Can Companies Really Feel Their Way to Success? Lauren Garris, Client Relationship Manager, UNC Executive Development.
[6] Annie McKee. "How to hire for emotional intelligence." Feb. 5, 2016. Harvard Business Review.

people's needs, which means they are unable to meet those needs or inspire people to act.

Employees in compassionate organizations are being trained in the skills required to apply EQ in their workplace. To work effectively with their peers and the organizations they work for, to derive the greatest return on their people investment.

When I conduct EQ training, we begin by addressing the four stages of EI that need to be achieved in sequential order, for the individual to become emotionally intelligent. These four stages of EI development are:

❶ **Self-Awareness:** This requires that you are aware of your feelings and emotions. It's a way of asking "How am I doing?" Self-awareness entails being able to identify why you are feeling a certain way, by understanding the underlying root causes.

One way that I train executives and professionals to gain a keener self-awareness is to have them answer the question: "Would you hire yourself?" I urge them to develop a compelling **Unique Value Proposition**, as a way to define and distinguish their competitive differentiation. An exercise that I have them conduct is to craft a sales script to effectively sell themselves to themselves. Sound odd? Okay, I get it. After all, it is not something you'd normally (or perhaps EVER) think of doing.

Well, hear me out. If they (you) provide the product, service, experience... that YOU need, would you hire them (YOU?) to deliver it? If the answer is a resounding "YES!" then that's fantastic. But can you say why? Write down what experiences, expertise, skills, training, language proficiency, qualities, characteristics, values you hold that form the essence of your personal reputational brand. What is it that makes you invaluable, unique, and memorable?

Defining your attributes thus really forces you to write down what sets you apart.

But...are you really being honest with yourself?

Would you EVER admit that you would NOT hire yourself? Of course not! Honestly, no one ever tells me they wouldn't hire themselves. That's the selective perception we all carry within ourselves. We see what we want to see and that is most often the case when we are conducting self-reflection.

It's a heightened sense of self-worth. I've had many clients declare they are an expert in their field. But...are you? How do you define that/quantify "EXPERTISE?"? What do you do that is unlike anything your competitors can offer? Often my executive coaching entails conducting an individual audit whereby I interview a select few (5-7) individuals that person has worked with, managed and/or reported to, or are close friends or serve on some volunteer basis or a Trade organization. I ask those folks what their personal experiences are with that individual.

Have you ever created a new process or workflow? Have you developed an entirely new product or created a new service? Do you excel at customer care? Do you really understand what it takes to serve clients? Do you treat your employees or peers like true business partners or the dreaded "asset?" Do co-workers come to YOU looking for help? What are your 3-4 success stories that you would use to describe what sets you apart from others in the same industry as you who possess or have possessed the same/similar job titles?

Do you possess some knowledge or have you gone through training that makes you unique? If you can't answer any of these questions with a resounding "Yes!" then you are NOT exceptional. You're what is referred to as a "Me Too" offering, and THAT is not "remarkable" as Seth Godin likes to say.

Your uniqueness and thus competitive advantage comes from the collective set of attributes that no one else can claim or emulate. Each of us is a unique combination of skills, background and experiences that no one else possesses. Your brand "fingerprint" as it were. So, go ahead and try to honestly sell yourself to yourself. Despite our selection perception, we are still our own toughest critics.

Why We Lie to Ourselves, And How to Stop.

Think about the times you have lied to yourself and/or to others. Why did you do it? A major behavioral trait that comes into question with respect to emotional awareness as the first stage of EI is understanding why we lie to ourselves.

I have found that as a business coach and executive trainer, my clients lie to ourselves (at work) for many of (if not all of) the same reasons that we lie to ourselves (and others) in our home life. There are in fact **FIVE** (5) key reasons why we lie to ourselves:

1. Conflict Avoidance: It's always easier to make the seemingly harmless little white lie such as: "Yes, I will definitely call you to schedule a lunch date" than it is to be cornered into a potentially confrontational stance we're forced to make: "No, honestly I don't like you and will never follow up with you."

2. Procrastination: Perhaps we lie to others and ourselves as a source of procrastination. "I'll be sure to get on that right away" can be translated into procrastination-speak as: "I'll wait until the very last possible moment, then I will be forced to rush to get it done and deliver potentially sub-par quality work." Or one of my personal favorites: "No I don't have a business succession / risk mitigation plan, but I promise I'll write that just as soon as I … [fill in any of your typical excuses for procrastination here."]

3. Arrogance: We lie because we are arrogant enough to believe we are superior to others. One example that I have heard countless times from business owners goes something like this: "I don't need a strategic plan (or coaching). I've been doing this for [fill in the amount of time in years.] I will forget more about my business in a year than you can EVER hope to learn."

4. Gain an Advantage/Benefit: We lie in order to benefit or gain from a situation. To gain some perspective, review the **Selfish Lying Matrix**. Depending on what is at stake we lie to gain or avoid material things or to gain/avoid the loss of social standing.

Selfish Lying Matrix

What is at stake	Gaining	Avoiding
Material	Gaining Advantage	Avoiding Punishment
Social	Gaining Esteem	Avoiding Embarrassment

5. Helping Others: The motivation for lying can and often does come from the altruistic intent of helping others.

Saving Face

'*Face*' is a term used to indicate public respect given to another person. 'Saving face' is thus a term used to describe helping others to maintain the respect of others and to avoid embarrassment.

This past semester, I taught a course on International Consumer Behavior to French students of ISM on a summer in New York semester at Baruch College. Through my teaching students in this international program, I discovered that different cultures have very specific rules about the degree of face-saving that is required, and how it should be done.

This is especially true when comparing Eastern "collectivist" (Asian) cultures where the group is always placed first before the individual's needs, with Western "individualistic" cultures where the wants, needs, and desires of the individual are often prioritized ahead of the group.

One way we help others to save face is more about not telling the truth rather than overtly lying. If we meet a person with bad breath, for example, most would avoid pointing out the problem. Beyond being 'economical with the truth', the lies we tell to save face may be couched in euphemisms and other vague statements as we try to help others feel good while we try to avoid telling big lies ourselves.

For great insight on the act and significance of lying, I urge you to watch **Pamela Meyer**, author of "Liespotting" and the TED Global 2011 talk entitled: *How to Spot a Liar*. She argues that lying is a "co-operative" act in which you need someone else to believe the lie. In 2010, lies cost the US $997 billion in corporate fraud. Taken to the extreme, lies can betray a country and jeopardize its safety as we are finding out with the Trump Administration's repeated acts of stealth and deception. [7]

Those (Not So) Little "White Lies"

Perhaps to reconcile what we know is unethical or anti-social behavior, we justify our lies as only little "White Lies." Not much harm in those, right?

---

[7] www.ted.com/talks/pamela_meyer_how_to_spot_a_liar#t-171862

What happens when our little white lies become so frequent that we lose our sense of integrity entirely along the way?

The larger societal impact of cheating and dishonesty.

Think that all those seemingly little, harmless lies "don't add up?" Guess again. We tend to think that people are either honest or dishonest. We like to believe that most people are virtuous, except for a few bad apples. If this were true, society could easily fix its problems with cheating and dishonesty. HR Departments could screen for cheaters when hiring. As it is, lying is a prevalent behavior of individuals faced with the tremendous stress of making their application look as appealing as possible for employment when job vacancies are not easy to come by. Dishonesty in professionals from financial advisers to building contractors could be identified quickly and branded with a Scarlet "**C**" for cheater and thus avoided. Cheaters in sports and other arenas would be easy to spot.

But that's not how dishonesty works. Research shows that everyone has the capacity to be dishonest, and almost everybody cheats from time to time just a little. Except for a few outliers at the top and bottom, the behavior of almost everyone is driven by two opposing motivations.

On the one hand, we want to benefit from cheating and gain as much reward, glory, benefit as possible. On the other, we want to view ourselves as being an honest, honorable person. Sadly, it is this kind of small-scale mass cheating, not the high-profile cases, that is most corrosive to society. [8]

If we know we're doing it, then why do we do it?

So, why don't we stop ourselves from lying?

There is a phrase in psychology called: "**Head trash**." Research reveals that for all people, approximately 65% of all the things we say to ourselves about ourselves is…NEGATIVE. Perhaps we lie as a mechanism to deal with this self-inflected psychological damage on some level.

---

[8] **Dan Arielly** "The Honest Truth About Dishonesty."

- We HEAR what we WANT to hear;
- We SEE what we WANT to see; and
- We BELIEVE what we WANT to believe.

What can you do to catch yourself in the act and stop lying as a self-improvement "best practice?"

For starters, strive to understand the reasons why you might be inclined to lie and use this in detecting the deception you practice.

If you are trying to get to the truth with someone who may be lying, you can help them avoid lying by helping them see it as a 'little deceit' that's not worth defending.

If you are a parent, you can help your children adopt the value that lying is bad altogether, rather than punishing them for lying. If you are a manager, create an organizational culture of honesty by praising your people for telling the truth. They will lie and cover up potentially embarrassing or damaging problems, which only helps organizations thrive.

❷ **Self-Management**: Once you identify the causes for your emotions, self-management entails beginning to control your emotions. Self-management requires one to possess the ability to ask "Why am I feeling this way?" It should lead to a deeper understanding as to what caused those feelings and how one should feel in that situation. Such self-analysis is a critical component of getting one's feelings "in check".

Emotional Regulation

Emotional Regulation is an aspect of self-regulation that involves an individual being able to:

- Identify and modify the emotions you feel.
- *Surface acting*: putting on a face. There are times when you simply cannot convey the emotions you are feeling. That is when "faking it" comes into play.
- Venting: open displays of emotion. Situations dictate when and to what degree venting is appropriate.

- People in good moods make better decisions, are more creative, and help motivate others. Thus, there are multiple reasons why self-regulation is needed to remain in balance.
- Emotional states affect employee levels, especially when discussing customer service.
- Negative feelings lead to a higher likelihood of deviant workplace behaviors.
- As a result, there has been an increase in the use of "happiness" coaches in organizations like AmEx, UBS, and KPMG.

❸ **Social Awareness:** This entails being aware of how the people around you are feeling. In order to be successful at being socially aware, one must possess empathy and caring for the people they work with/for. It absolutely requires one to ask how others are doing, but at a deeper level requires you to pay attention to the many non-verbal cues that people send out that may contradict how they say they are doing. How do people respond to you?

Ever wonder why the statements made by senior-level employees fairly high up in organizations about the culture where they work is so out of whack with the reality of that organization's actual culture. Well, it has to do with the fact that they are organizational above (and removed) from many of the day to day operations of the organization. They often do not interact with the organization's customers, nor do they have much of any engagement with front-line operations-based staff.

It never fails to amuse me when I speak with Senior executives about the state of affairs in their organization, then speak with lower level employees. High level officials are blissfully unaware and uncaring of the challenges facing lower level staff, their needs, wants, and desires.

Senior Management is often in effect socially clueless and blind to the world that is the actual organization. It is often as if there are two entirely different cultures that exist. You may wonder how such organizations can exist given how out of touch their high-ranking employees are. The truth is, they can't. Thus, the justification for empowering employees and giving them greater control over their own work.

Do You Care What Others Think of You?

A strong motivator in social awareness is caring what others think about you. As an executive trainer and business coach, I am fortunate to be invited to give talks to many different groups of professionals on all sorts of career and professionalism topics. One of my absolute favorites is on building an amazing personal brand by *forging powerful relationships* for career and professional success.

I realize there is an underlying assumption at play with personal branding which is this: you build a compelling brand because you CARE what others think about you.

This goes a long way towards building strong relationships forged on mutual trust, caring and benefit.

Therefore, the question that begs asking is this: **Do you act in such a way that demonstrates you care about others**?

For example, a few months ago I met a fellow member of my local Chamber of Commerce for a "get to know each other" chat. During our conversation, she mentioned she wanted to introduce me to a senior executive in her firm that might like to know about my employee training. I said great. And waited weeks then months for her to make an introduction. Nothing.

I then saw her at another Chamber event in which I actually presented to the group on building powerful relationships. So, I mentioned it again to her. She cavalierly responded: "Email me a reminder." I did. Weeks (then months) later…nothing. No response.

Can you guess what I might say when someone in our professional circle asks me about her? This behavior speaks to an individual's professionalism, commitment, follow through…or lack thereof! Which is really all about individual personality "brand characteristics." It goes much deeper than simply this example:

- Do you respond to calls and emails to others, even folks you don't know?

- Do you send thank you emails (or postcards) for all sorts of reasons?

- Do you share interesting articles, and send people links to videos/TED talks they might be interested in or can benefit from?

- Do you go out of your way to introduce people that can benefit from knowing each other? Or, if someone goes out of their way to help you do you reciprocate or at a minimum acknowledge their gesture with a thank you?

Or how about this? Back in May I reached out to my State Bar Association to offer to conduct a specific training program to their members. Over the course of THREE months, I attempted (unsuccessfully) to contact not one, not two...but EIGHT members of their "Leadership" team.

Not a single individual there responded. I had spent months developing a special program on how attorneys can benefit from utilizing emotional intelligence to influence their peers, opposing counsel, judges, and juries.

In short...are you a taker or a giver? **Do people like, respect, and trust you?** To see how your reputational brand stands up, why not test what YOU think OTHERS think of you against what they actually think of you?

How? ASK THEM! Start by writing down a list of **5-6 core personality trait brand characteristics** you want to be known for (Ex. reliable, honest, kind, trustworthy, knowledgeable, etc.)

Next, ask 5-6 of your closest friends, peers, clients, co-workers...to provide a similar list of your professional brand attributes. The degree to which their collective responses match/coincide with yours shows how authentic you are, and whether you are being true to your reputational brand.

If their results are a match to your list...**congratulations!** You are living your brand. If not...then that's a golden opportunity to enhance your relationships. Further, you should make sure your online brand is consistent with how people engage you face to face. Be sure to regularly assess your online brand (conduct an online brand audit) of your reputational brand.

Is Arrogance Limiting Your Career Potential?

Do you suffer from "Arrogance?" Is your arrogance hurting your career and/or your business?

Arrogance is defined as: "...an insulting way of thinking or behaving that comes from believing that you are better, smarter, or more important than other people. Showing an offensive attitude of superiority." [9]

Arrogance entails propping yourself up - whether it's through public displays or to yourself. It often involves knocking others down, at the same time. It is generally defined as all of the following:

- *The act or habit of making undue claims in an overbearing manner;*
- *That species of pride which consists in exorbitant claims of rank, dignity, estimation, or power, or which exalts the worth or importance of the person to an undue degree; and*
- *Proud contempt of others.*

Other names for arrogance are: egotism, conceit, grandiosity, and self-importance. I see arrogance in my consulting practice on a near daily basis. It manifests itself in my clients' refusal to admit they have blind spots or areas of weakness that can and often hinder their ability to achieve optimal levels of performance.

A perfect example is when a business owner or Senior level executive invites me in to discuss their challenges. Invariably the discussion gravitates to their people. Such conversations invariably spiral into some permutation of: "my people are lazy, unmotivated, not dedicated enough, don't work hard enough, don't share my passion for my business..." The arrogance inherent in such a 'blame game' is, the individual finds everyone else except themselves at fault.

Ancient Greek literature refers to such behavior as **hubris,** a form of arrogance in which a person thinks himself to be higher in status than other ordinary mortals. In other words, a god. Such behavior typically can be traced back to an individual's early childhood and the fear of their OWN **vulnerability** to negative perceptions that others have of them, such as:

---

[9] www.merriam-webster.com/dictionary/arrogant.

- *Being vulnerable to any kind of criticism or disapproval.*
- *Any perceived weakness, failing or imperfection is undesirable and unacceptable.*
- *If I show any of my **real** weaknesses, failings or imperfections, it could be disastrous.*[10]

> "Nothing so obstinately stand in the way of all sorts of progress as pride of opinion. While nothing is so foolish and baseless." – J.G. Holland

Hence, showing vulnerability in the eyes of others becomes unacceptable and frightening. The coping mechanism these individuals employ to manage their fear is to *manipulate* others' perceptions—to ensure that there is never anything for them to disapprove of or criticize.

Perhaps you achieved a fair measure of success or were given a high-ranking position, which led you to take on an inflated sense of yourself. This likely has manifested itself in a heightened sense of your own self-importance which is the classic definition of arrogance.

HOW TO TELL IF YOU TRULY ARE ARROGANT.

Following is a short list of questions you can and should ask yourself, to gauge the degree of hubris you possess. Take a minute to answer the following questions either as either "YES or NO." You have to answer truthfully.

1. Do you find yourself often dismissing the ideas of others off-hand and without consideration, because you think you are more experienced, seasoned, or possess a better insight or their insights cannot help you?
2. Do you assume that your business cannot possibly lose market share from that upstart that lacks your size, resources, and time spent in business?
3. Do you think your employees perform at high enough levels of productivity, and do not require additional training, motivation, rewards and recognition from you?
4. Do you avoid soliciting ideas from your employees, friends, family, peers as a general practice?

---

[10] http://hanofharmony.com/the-dangers-of-pride-and-arrogance.

5. Are you confident you know everything there is to know about your business, the industry you compete in, your clients, vendors, and employees? **HINT**: If you answered YES to this, drop your pen right now, because you ARE arrogant. There simply is NO way we can know everything there is to know about EVERYTHING.

6. Would you consider reaching out to an outsider (a coach, mentor, consultant, adviser, confidant) to help you improve your professional acumen and business operations?

7. When was the last time you said the words "I WAS WRONG" or "I'M SORRY?"

By answering any of questions one through six in the affirmative, you likely possess a degree of arrogance, which may pose a threat to your career, professional and business goals.

> **"An arrogant person considers himself perfect. This is the chief harm of arrogance. It interferes with a person's main task in life – becoming a better person." - Leo Tolstoy**

Why?

Arrogance can have an extremely debilitating effect on those people that are incapable of seeing the value in others.

For starters, arrogance can lead to **complacency**. Arrogance can lead to the false belief that one is capable of resolving all the challenges one encounters in these constantly changing times without assistance from others.

Excessive pride can cause one to **make careless and unnecessary mistakes** due to a lack of wise judgement. You may trust too much in your instincts and abilities, underestimate the situation or the capabilities of your competitors, overestimate the loyalty you have built with your clients, employees, vendors and other stakeholders.

Arrogance can **cloud your judgement** and make you **lose touch with reality**, which will always lead to failure.

Being arrogance can lead us not to seek out and heed the advice of others and to the extreme can and will serve to **alienate the people you trust most and rely on**. Arrogance is a personality trait that is universally despised.

OKAY. I MAY BE ARROGANT, BUT WHAT IS THERE TO DO?

If you ever find yourself exhibiting such behavior and truly wish to stop, here are a few suggestions I work with my clients to implement on a routine basis.

1. Give meaningful compliments by citing specific accomplishments that others have achieved. Don't say "You did great work." That's meaningless. Cite specific examples of the challenge they faced, the action(s) they took, and the results achieved.
2. Learn to ask questions, then listen HARD! Listening at 100% and being FULLY engaged is truly one of the hardest things to do but is so rewarding.
3. Give credit to others, rather than taking it all for yourself.
4. Admit when you're wrong. It is NOT a sign of weakness, but rather of incredible strength.
5. Laugh at yourself. Don't be so quick to take offense.

Remember you have limitations, you're not perfect so you can constantly learn from experiences AND OTHERS if only you open yourself up to the possibility of achieving true growth and becoming a better person.

❹ **Social Management**: Begin to effectively manage/control relationships by being more in tune with other peoples' feelings.

In summary, EI is a person's ability to effectively perceive the emotions they are feeling and the emotions of others. It demands an understanding as to the causes and meaning of these emotions, AND the ability to regulate one's own emotions as well as having a positive impact on others.

There are certain considerations that need to be taken into account when considering implementing EQ training as a component of your people's training and professional development. For starters, there is a very high direct correlation between possessing a high level of EI and achieving job/career success.

Organizations are beginning to use EI with greater frequency in their hiring practices and employee training, given the growing importance of team-based work and employees being able to work effectively with one another. Despite the many benefits of employing EI, it has not yet achieved universal organizational embrace.

It is often quite amusing to see how utterly unaware managers are with respect to their (lack of) social management. When I was hired to lead the marketing efforts for a major cable MSO in the NY Region reporting to the Divisional President, he explained to me that he needed me to take over much of the day to day communications with our Corporate HQ in Virginia. When I asked him why, he explained that he had already burned quite a few bridges, and needed me to repair damaged relationships with our Region. He was aware of his own social management challenges, and needed to repair our standing in order to accomplish his ambitious growth strategies by enlisting their support.

As a field of study and practical guide for organizations, EQ has many supporters and detractors. Therefore, there are considerable differences in perspective on its efficacy, depending on who you consult with. Lastly, there are as yet no commonly accepted tests to gauge one's measure/degree of EQ. Still, the power associated with being able to control one's own emotions and have a positive effect on others they work with cannot be overstated.

EI Is Implemented 'Big-Time' at Google

In 2006, Chade-Meng Tan, a Google engineer who was the company's 107th employee when he joined Google in 1999 looked to develop a program to train his fellow Googlers to be more mindful in their lives.

He wanted to train people to become more aware of their emotions, more compassionate toward others, more able to build sustainable relationships, and, ultimately, able to contribute to world peace. Or at the very least peace and harmony in Google's workplace.

Tan assembled a team that included consultants, a Stanford scientist, and Marc Lesser, a Zen teacher with an MBA and entrepreneurial experience. The first "Search Inside Yourself" two-day course was taught to Googlers in 2007. It wasn't long after that the influential curriculum led to Tan's appointment as

Google's **Jolly Good Fellow**. His position requires him to "enlighten minds, open hearts, create world peace." What an amazing job title.

An estimated 1,500 Googlers are expected to go through the training this year, while thousands wait for future open seats. In 2012, Tan and his team decided to make the course available to organizations and communities outside of Google. The Search Inside Yourself Leadership Institute (SIYLI) was launched as a nonprofit, while Tan's book, *Search Inside Yourself*, became endorsed by the Dalai Lama and former American President Jimmy Carter.

Only organizations that are mature and evolved in their informal culture care enough about their people to offer such training on EQ as Google does. Think about the innovation and creativity that is unleashed at Google from its people possessing the emotional intelligence to understand themselves and their peers.

And EI is not only embraced by Google. Many world-class organizations such as BMW, Coca-Cola, L'Oreal, and Shell understand that EQ provides real, bottom-line value and positive impact. That's why they make it a strategic priority and invest in it as a mandatory skill to train its people. Think how much productivity gain can be achieved in your organization by making an investment in your people's EI with training, as Google and other compassionate organizations make.

There is a significant body of research to indicate that the strongest leaders all possess significant EI.

"When asked to define the ideal leader, many would emphasize traits such as intelligence, toughness, determination, and vision—the qualities traditionally associated with leadership. Such skills are necessary but insufficient qualities for the leader. Often left off the list are softer, more personal qualities— but they are also essential. **Although a certain degree of analytical and technical skill is a minimum requirement for success, studies indicate that emotional intelligence may be the key attribute that distinguishes outstanding performers from those who are merely adequate.**"[11]

RELYING ON PERSONALITY AND VALUES

Personality is defined as:

---

[11] https://hbr.org/2004/01/what-makes-a-leader.

> **"The dynamic organization within the individual of those psychophysical systems that determine his unique adjustments to his environment."** - *Gordon Alport*

Some excellent personality assessment tools you may wish to investigate include:

• The Small Business Administration website: www.sba.gov/starting_business/startup/areyouready.html
• *Change Style Indicator* from MHS Assessments can be used to show how receptive your employees are to change. Change Style Indicator˚ is a leadership assessment tool that was designed to measure an individual's preferred style in approaching and addressing change. It provides leaders with insights on personal preferences for managing through change and provides context for how those around them might perceive and respond to their preferred style.[12]
• Personality type/career assessment tools:

  ▪ Myers Briggs Type Indicator (MBTI)
  ▪ MAPP Career Test: www.assessment.com
  ▪ The 16 personality types: [www.personalitypage.com/high-level.html]
  ▪ *Keirsey Assessment* [www.keirsey.com] The Keirsey Temperament Sorter is a powerful 70 question personality instrument that helps individuals discover their personality type. The KTS-II is based on Keirsey Temperament Theory™, published in the books, Please Understand Me® and Please Understand Me II, by Dr. David Keirsey.[13]
  ▪ *The Birkman Method* (https://birkman) is a behavioral assessment (not a personality test) developed by Roger Birkman that shows you what you do. This assessment tool shows you your usual behavior (your positive style/your visible strengths), your motivational needs (which can be quite different than your usual style and is

---

[12] https://tap.mhs.com/ChangeStyleIndicator.aspx
[13] http://www.keirsey.com/sorter/register.aspx.

often invisible to others) and your likely stress behaviors when your go unmet.[14]

- *DISC Tool* DISC is a behavior assessment tool based on the **DISC** theory of psychologist William Moulton Marston, which centers on assessing four different behavioral traits: **d**ominance, **i**nducement, **s**ubmission, and **c**ompliance and is typically used for evaluating **SALES** professionals [htttps://discprofile.com] Also is said to stand for **D**ominance, **I**nfluence, **S**teadiness, and Conscientiousness.

The Myers Briggs 16 Personality Dynamics

- Extraverted (**E**) vs. Introverted (**I**)

  Es are outgoing and sociable; **Is** are quiet and shy.
- Sensing (**S**) vs. Intuitive (**N**)

  S are practical and prefer order and structure over chaos and undefined roles and situations. **N** look at/see the big picture and tend to gloss over details.
- Thinking (**T**) vs. Feeling (**F**)

  T apply logic to problem-solving. **F** rely on their own personal values and emotions to guide their decision-making.
- Judging (**J**) vs. Perceiving (**P**)

  J value control over situations and prefer order. **P** are flexible and spontaneous, and tend to perform well in undefined roles and uncertain circumstances.

  INTJ are visionaries who possess original minds and great drive.

THE "BIG 5" PERSONALITY TRAITS

Today, many researchers and personality psychologists believe that there are five core dimensions of personality referred to as the "Big 5" personality traits. Evidence of this theory has been growing for many years, beginning with the research of D. W. Fiske (1949) and later expanded upon by other researchers including Norman (1967), Smith (1967), Goldberg (1981), and McCrae & Costa (1987). [15]

---

[14] http://www.mycallingiq.com/what-is-the-birkman-method.

[15] www.verywell.com/the-big-five-personality-dimensions-2795422.

Those five traits are:

- **Extraversion**: How comfortable we are with forging and maintaining relationships. With more and more work being completed in ad-hoc groups/teams that form within organizations to work on specific projects, a key measure of success is the ability to lead and/or participate in Teams across the organization.

  The growing importance of Team-based work increases as organizations look to connect geographically dispersed workforces on virtual Teams. Thus, extraversion assists workers in being able to connect with others in productive relationships that extend well beyond their own Functional areas (Marketing, Sales, HR, etc.) in cross-functional teams comprised of employees from different cultures, backgrounds, and upbringing.

- **Agreeableness**: How warm and trusting are you? To go along, you have to GET along. Are you someone that others can work for and with, in constructive, productive work relationships? Being technically proficient (good at your job) is no longer good enough. We also need to be able to form meaningful, constructive work relationships.

  This personality trait includes attributes such as: trust, altruism, kindness, and affection. These are known as 'pro-social' behaviors. People who are high in agreeableness tend to be more cooperative, while those low in this trait tend to be more competitive and even manipulative.

- **Conscientiousness**: Defined as people who are responsible, dependable, organized, and persistent. This trait demands an intense focus on completing the work. Are you someone that can be trusted to get things done? Features of this dimension include high levels of thoughtfulness. Conscientious individuals possess good impulse control and are goal-directed. High conscientiousness individuals tend to be organized and extremely mindful of the details required to achieve success.

- **Neuroticism**: Neuroticism has to do with individuals focusing on the experience of negative emotions. Individuals who fall in the neurotic category tend to be more prone to mood swings and emotional reactivity.

- **Openness to Experiences**: Do you possess a range of interests and a fascination with novelty? Those who possess an openness to experience are more inclined to appreciate art and beauty, and are receptive to having new experiences. Given the uncertain times we live in, those individuals that embrace new opportunities to learn and grow are often better suited to contribute in meaningful ways to the organizations they commit to.

Respect is EARNED, Not GIVEN.

It is a truism that people don't do business with you because of what you do or how you do it. Rather they decide whether to engage with you based on **how you make them FEEL about you**.

Check out Simon Sinek's TED talk from 2009 "**Start with Why**" for a primer:

People making emotional connections with you or being repelled by you can be a blessing or a curse, depending on how you act in your professional and personal relationships.

I've noticed a proliferation in shall we say less than professional behavior the past few years. This less than desirable behavior seems to be reaching a "tipping scale" issue as more and more people face time constraints, work-life balance issues, attempt to start their own businesses, and organizations build work forces comprised of employees spanning the FIVE generations: Matures, Boomers, Generation X, Generation Y/Millennials, and iGeneration/Gen Zs.

So, following is a VERY short list I prepared of Do's and Don'ts to ensure the reputational credit you have forged through valuable relationships remains untarnished in these challenging times:

1. **Be a (Relationship) Farmer, NOT a Hunter**: In relationship styles, the Hunter and the Farmer exist on the opposite ends of the human behavioral spectrum. The "hunter" aggressively seeks out new clients to conquer. This is called "The Hunt." Hunters love independence, and see each client gained as a conquest.

The Hunter approaches relationships as a "**zero-sum gain**." For them to "WIN" someone else must "LOSE." For these types of folks, it's all about the thrill of the (new client acquisition) hunt.

Call them rainmakers or whatever label helps you understand what makes them tick. JUST TRY NOT TO BE LIKE THEM. They are lone wolfs. They're not keen on nurturing existing client relationships. For them it's all about sealing the deal.

Then there are the *Farmers*. Their idea of relationship-building is all about planting seeds. They are nurturers by nature. They are genuinely concerned about the long-view approach to relationships. They make connections for others, share ideas, provide ideas and resources.

Farmers plant relationship seeds by checking in on people periodically, to see how they're doing. Chances are they're active in their communities, and do a lot of volunteer work. They coach, mentor, teach, advise. They epitomize true GIVING.

Clearly, very few people exhibit solely ONE type of behavior all the time such as these two ends of the continuum. But it will help guide you in your relationships if you ask yourself which type you are behaving like when you engage others.

1. **Our ANTI-Social Media**: your online brand should match the in-person demeanor you portray. Do you speak online in such a way that emulates your face-to-face persona. If I read what you wrote online and then heard you speak in person, would I recognize both as the SAME person?

In other words, are you being true to who you are and thus your "brand?" When you post, it is important to understand the different types of social media, how they are used, and who is using them.

For example, there is a huge war being raged on LinkedIn right now by the traditional users who believe it should only be used for business-related relationship building. I admit, I'm one of those people. Then there are others who use LinkedIn for socializing, as an extension of Facebook. They post images asking to vote on their best profile picture, post announcements of their graduations, etc. It's NOT.

As a general rule of thumb, avoid making statements online that are incendiary, insensitive, and divisive. It helps to NOT discuss sensitive issues that can polarize, such as race, sex, religion, politics, etc. You say this is purely common sense? I disagree.

It seems like social media can be used to bring people together or push them apart, but it is all too easy to hide behind an online account and say things that can only damage the relationships you have worked so hard to build.

1. **Be Responsive and Accessible**: In full disclosure, this is a really big "PET PEEVE" turn off behavior of mine.

When people attempt to call you or email you, assuming they are looking to work with you in some capacity at least have the decency to respond. The *"If I ignore them they'll go away"* mindset is actually an incredibly passive-aggressive behavior, and quite insensitive. It's one thing to ignore a telemarketer or spammer. We all hate and therefore avoid those types of behavior. I get that.

But it is entirely another thing to avoid someone (whether you know them or not) that has done significant research on how their service can help your organization. Let's say they make a concerted effort to have a discussion with you, yet you refuse to respond to their numerous inquiries.

You might be thinking: "Can't they get the hint?" Ask yourself: "If I were in that person's shoes, is that how I would like to be treated?" Call them back or respond to their emails. It can be as simple as "No thank you. I'm not interested."

The same can be said for NOT stringing people along. If you do not foresee a scenario in which you would work with them, hire them, or engage their services, tell them up front. It does no one a bit of good to lead people.

I'm sure I've missed quite a few. What are some of your pet peeve *relationship-killers*?

Another way to look at human behavior.

Takers, Givers, and Matchers

Organizational psychologist Adam Grant surveyed over 30,000 people in organizations across industries all over the world. He found that all people can be grouped into the following three types of behaviors: 1) Takers; 2) Givers; and 3) Matchers. Takers approach relationships with the mindset: "What can YOU do for ME?" while Givers are thinking: "What can I do for YOU?" [16]

Matchers approach relationships in a *quid pro quo* fashion by thinking: "I'll do something for you, if you do something for me." If someone gives to them, they give back. If they encounter a Taker, they take in return. Not surprisingly, most people fall under the Matcher category.

Grant's findings are extremely enlightening from an organizational performance perspective and a blue print for how to build more compassion into the workplace. Givers are both the least and most productive employees. They are often so busy helping others that they often struggle to get their own work done. Givers sacrifice themselves but in the process, they make their organizations a better place to work.

By any measure of performance organizations with a culture of Givers perform at a higher level, whether it be financial performance, customer service ratings, whatever. Takers rise and fall quickly, most often at the hands of Matchers. For organizations that wish to optimize their people's relationships and thus productivity, they need to change their culture to accommodate the Givers.

Organizations can take three immediate steps to nurture their Givers: 1) Protect Givers from burnout; 2) encourage help-seeking; and 3) build a workforce of Givers. Note that this will require your organization to begin aggressively weeding out the Takers. The negative impact of Takers has 2-3 times the negative impact to the organization as one Giver. [17]

Replace 'What's in it for me?' Selfishness with Giving Selflessness.

I've spent the past nine years as a business coach and management consultant. In that time, I have had the pleasure and good fortune to work with 350 clients and give talks to over 15,000 individuals. I've attended thousands of networking events. One trend that is quite disturbing is the selfish behavior

---

[16] www.ted.com/talks/adam_grant_are_you_a_giver_or_a_taker.

[17] Adam Grant, TED talk "Are you a giver or a taker?" www.ted.com/talks/adam_grant_are_you_a_giver_or_a_taker#t-52398.

exhibited by solopreneurs, entrepreneurs, the self-employed, and professionals who network from a VERY selfish "**What's in it for me**" approach.

I'd like to propose a new approach that will enable you to build stronger relationships based on trust, caring, and constantly delivering value to others.

Following are six practices you can employ to build your professional EQ. If you have to take a selfish approach to giving, then trust me when I say... caring for others and putting others first will pay off for you in the long run through more valuable relationships.

1. **Share Information** – Pass along relevant articles, business resources, TED talks, videos, and information to the people in your network that you think can benefit most from this information.

Whenever you come across information that you think can be interesting, useful, or relevant to people you know, then by all means you should SHARE the knowledge with them. It will have a boomerang effect, and lead others to want to reciprocate...or NOT. That's also fine. Giving should not come with strings attached.

2. **Don't Hoard Your Expertise** – If you have insights, experience and expertise in certain areas, share the 'wealth.' Becoming known for your 'Subject Matter Expertise' will lead others to seek out your knowledge, and that can be invaluable. By doing so you become a BRAND that is known for helping others gain insights and solve problems.

3. **Be a "Facilitator" By Connecting Others** – Do you know those people who are always working to introduce people in their networks to each other that they think can help each other? They are the type of people that others enjoy spending time with, and are always speaking positively about.

How can you become that kind of person? Simple. By converting friends, peers, co-workers and professional contacts in your network into your very own tribe of raving fans (hat tip to Ken Blanchard & Sheldon Bowles) by constantly thinking who you can connect.

4. **Take Someone Under Your Wing** – In my early 20s when I relocated to Washington, DC to accept employment as a Recruiter in a national placement firm, I was fortunate to have someone much older and wiser gentleman by the name of Barry Locke take me under his wing.

Barry would take me out to lunch, share his life experiences and provide a sounding board for me to bounce ideas off of. He taught me the value of building strong relationships, being focused on serving others and coaching/mentoring. He was kind and patient, and never passed judgement. In so many ways Barry helped me to figure out how to navigate the challenges of work. Who can YOU coach/mentor?

5. **Practice Emotional Intelligence** – you may have noticed that a relatively large portion of this book is dedicated to EQ. There's a reason for that. EQ is the driving force that enables organizations to thrive by ensuring their culture is strong.

> **"Emotional intelligence isnot the opposite of inmtelligence it is not t he triumph of heart over head – it is the nique intersection of both." - David Caruso**

6. **Build Your Reputational Brand** – By becoming known for your sharing and thoughtfulness, you build a powerfully engaging personal and professional brand. And why does personal branding matter these days? As it turns out, there are many reasons why you want (NEED) a compelling brand.

For starters, you can reduce the effort required by others to understand you, your needs, background, skills…what makes you "tick!" Your brand defines your QUALITIES/ABILITIES, and enables you to present your professional attributes.

Further, it gives others the chance to "connect" with your brand, and at the same time, by being known as someone that looks out for others, it's a sign of your perceived quality and PRESTIGE, and lastly…your brand help others to organize all of their knowledge about you and their collective experiences interacting with you.

So. There you have it. Make your relationships truly matter. Don't be the sales version of a hunter, always looking to conquer that next prospect. Avoid the Takers. Instead be a farmer that plants the seeds of valuable relationships in all the things you do for others. Give!

The negative impact that Takers can have on organizations is toxic. When taken to the extreme these Taker individuals are referred to as narcissists, which is one of the three behavioral traits of the Dark Triad.

BEWARE OF THE DARK TRIAD

In the Dark Triad, there are three primary personality tendencies that showcase the dark side of human behavior and can lead to significant organizational challenges thus preventing a compassionate culture from taking root. Compassionate organizations are constantly on the look-out for, and fight to prevent, these three deviant behaviors from taking root in their organizations: Machiavellianism, Narcissism, and Psychopathy.

Machiavellianism

People who tend to lean towards Machiavellian behavior are pragmatists, to the extreme. These types of people MUST maintain their emotional distance from others. They tend to have only superficial relationships with others, and relationships are developed for purely self-gain purposes.

They justify their behavior by subscribing to the belief that "the end justifies the means."

Their behavior at work and in their personal lives is predicated on the constant pursuit of power. People who practice such behavior derive enjoyment and fulfillment in manipulating others, in order to "win MORE." As such, Machiavellian people tend to be extremely persuasive.

Their constant need for power demands that such individuals act aggressively. Further, individuals who behave this way are much more likely to engage in counterproductive workplace behavior.

Narcissism

People who are classified as narcissists are self-centered, have an extremely high sense of their own self-worth, or a grandiose sense of their self-importance. They require excessive admiration from others which manifests in the workplace as a need for constant validation of their work and recognition.

Such individuals tend to be more charismatic than others, and taken to the extreme have a high sense of entitlement. The truly believe that they are owed and can/will lash out if they do not receive the perceived rewards they feel they are entitled to.

In summary, such individuals must be "LOVED!"

You must be tired of them. They're everywhere. Narcissists. And if you think there are more of them than ever, you're right. Research shows we are experiencing a narcissism epidemic.[18]

From Twenge and Campbell's research findings in The Narcissism Epidemic: Living in the Age of Entitlement:

"In data from 37,000 college students, narcissistic personality traits rose just as fast as obesity from the 1980s to the present, with the shift especially pronounced for women. The rise in narcissism is accelerating, with scores rising faster in the 2000s than in previous decades."

As Twenge and Campbell explain, it's a myth that narcissism is just "high self-esteem" or that underneath it all narcissists are insecure and overcompensating. Narcissists believe they really are awesome. How can you tell if someone is a narcissist? It's easy. Ask them. Research shows narcissists feel so good about themselves they don't mind admitting it. Narcissism can be quite beneficial in the short term. They make fantastic first impressions. In job interviews and starting new jobs, narcissists get results. And in youth, being a narcissist even makes you happier. Narcissists are more likely to become leaders and narcissists who obsessively work hard are more likely to get promoted.[19]

But the stuff that works for them so well in the short term proves lethal in the long term. That job interview is great but University of Pennsylvania professor Scott Barry Kaufman explains that after three weeks people regard narcissists as untrustworthy. And narcissists might become leaders but they're not good ones. And when prestige isn't on the line, most narcissists don't work that hard.

From <u>The Narcissism Epidemic: Living in the Age of Entitlement</u>:

"...college students with inflated views of themselves (who think they are better than they actually are) make poorer grades the longer they are in college. They are also more likely to drop out. In another study, students who flunked an introductory psychology course had by far the highest narcissism scores, and those who made A's had the lowest."

---

18 Eric Barker. June 8, 2017. "5 Scientific Secrets to handling a Narcissist." LinkedIn.
19 Eric Barker. June 8, 2017. "5 Scientific Secrets to handling a Narcissist." LinkedIn.

For a world-class example of narcissism, I introduce you to the former CEO of British Petroleum, Tony Hayward. During the 2010 Deep Water Horizon oil spill, the NY Times quoted him as saying to his fellow BP executives on April 29: "What the hell did we do to deserve this?" Umm…environmentalists and the families who lost loved ones who died in the explosion could ask the same question.

Weeks later on May 18th he was at it again: ""I think the environmental impact of this disaster is likely to be very, very modest." That same day, when asked about whether he was able to sleep at night in light of the oil spill's disastrous effects, he replied, "Of course I can."

On May 31st Hayward told reporters, "The first thing to say is I'm sorry." However, he continued, "We're sorry for the massive disruption it's caused their lives. There's no one who wants this over more than I do. I would like my life back." He got his wish. A month later he was fired.

Psychopathy

Psychopathy entails a lack of concern for other people. People who exhibit this trait lack guilt/remorse when their actions cause harm to others. There is inconclusive research about psychopathy and its impact on job performance. From a managerial perspective, this behavior can be identified by individuals who are caught using such 'hard influence' tactics as threats and manipulation.

When I worked for that large NY-based cable operator my boss, the President who had hired me to repair all the bridges he burned with Corporate was pushed out when our Region was taken over by Corporate. The Senior executive who was assigned to manage us (Joe) was very close personal friends with Ralph, one of our Management Team members. So, Joe assigned Ralph with the day to day operational responsibility of leading our team, thus taking over as boss.

Ralph was an alcoholic, a drug user, had several cases of sexual harassment filed by fellow employees and was the epitome of a psychopath. After one of our weekly staff meetings in which I questioned some of his decisions, he stormed into my office, slammed the door and threatened to "end me" if I contradicted him in public ever again. I went to HR, requested the incident be documented in our employee files and demanded action be taken. None was. Months later when a new Executive was assigned to lead our Division, all but one of our nine-member Management Team was downsized.

THE FUNCTION OF EMOTIONS IN ORGANIZATIONS

What if any role does emotion play within the context of organizations and organizational behavior?

In a word...*EVERYTHING!*

Emotions are a human condition. Organizations are comprised of human beings (ignoring robots, of course). Therefore, in a literal sense emotions shape and are shaped by organizational life. Employees bring to their work experience a wide range of emotions that engage with others' emotions. The outcome or end product of the interaction of an organization's peoples' emotions IS organizational behavior. Emotions drive an organization's ability to function and perform.

Emotions are an integral part of thinking, judgment, decision-making and other so-called rational organizational processes. Organizations don't act rationally, because PEOPLE DON'T ALWAYS ACT RATIONALLY.

How does it feel to work for an employer that treats its people extremely well or poorly? What does ongoing mass layoffs do to employee morale, that nebulous term used to describe an organization's collective human spirit? How does it feel when promotions and rewards are divvied out not on a performance basis (meritocracy) but purely as a result of who you know or have good relations with (nepotism)?

In an emotional labor study of Customer Service employees conducted by Michael Cossette and Ursula Hess, motivated employees suppress their emotions much less often at work. Thus, an employees' motivation helps them to adopt more authentic and honest feelings towards the organization's customers.

Research on the regulation of emotions has focused on two main strategies: *surface acting* and *deep acting* (Brotheridge & Lee, 2002, 2003; Diefendorff et al., 2005; Grandey, 2003). When surface acting, an employee modifies the observable aspects of the unsuitable, typically negative, emotion by suppressing its expression or by faking a positive affect (PA). In contrast, deep acting involves the management of one's inner feelings, in order to feel and express the required/appropriate emotion.[20]

Moreover, employees' who feel motivated are more likely to be positively impacted with emotional labor strategies, such as engagement, reward & recognition. Of tremendous importance, employees experienced much greater levels of job satisfaction when they were acting with more honest emotions. Translation? Employees are much more satisfied when they don't have to make an act out of caring about their clients.[21]

The field of research surrounding employee emotions has grown considerably in the past few decades to the point where there is an International Conference on Emotions in Organizational Life – Emonet. The 11th annual conference is scheduled for August 8-9, 2018 in Chicago, IL. Learn about it at www. emotionsnet.org

A study that was conducted at the Wharton School of Business found that keeping employees happy involves more than ping-pong tables and a private chef. "Employees who felt they worked in a loving, caring culture reported higher levels of satisfaction and teamwork," write researchers Sigal Barsade and Olivia O'Neill in Harvard Business Review. It turns out, happy employees show up for work more often, and their attitude impacts relationships with clients.[22]

Building a strong emotional culture not only requires transformational leaders who build strong relationships with their employees, but a powerful culture built on a strong history, a clear and positive vision and mission statement and a moral compass of ethical behavior.

Do emotions make us rational or irrational?

---

[20] "EMOTION REGULATION STRATEGIES AMONG CUSTOMER SERVICE EMPLOYEES: A MOTIVATIONAL APPROACH." Michael Cossette, Ursula Hess. Research on Emotion in Organizations. Chapter 12, page 331.
[21] "Emotion Regulation Strategies Among Customer Service Employees: A Motivational Approach." Michael Cossette, Ursula Hess. Research on Emotion in Organizations. Chapter 12, page 329.
[22] "Why you should care about your company's emotional culture." Feb. 14, 2014. Stephanie Vozza. Fast Company.

Recent research says showing emotions makes us MORE rational. Psychologists identify emotions as complex states involving our mind, body and the external_environment. As summarized by Stanford University's Elise Dan-Glausner and James Gross (2013), emotions are "patterned appraisals that lead us to coordinated changes across experiential, behavioral, and physiological response systems" (p. 832). We base our emotions on our perceptions of the events going on in and around us. In turn, our emotions lead us to show one or more patterns of behavior.[23]

Being able to understand and control your emotional responses are key skills that influence your relationships with others. People will stay away from you if you're constantly expressing negative emotions. You might even put your job security, relationships, and health at risk. Under the wrong circumstances, you could even lose your life, such as expressing road rage.

In summary, emotions enable us to make more informed decisions that benefit our organizations when we cull that information in order to successfully navigate the minefields of our own and others' behaviors.

Aligning Emotion with Information Enhances Decision-Making

Aligning emotions with information, and learning what that information is telling you, relieves that sense of failure at feeling an emotion, and can help leaders know how to deal with other people's emotional responses. Emotions are designed to give us data about ourselves and our environment to guide decision-making. The more information we have, the better equipped we are to make wise decisions and take effective action.[24]

If we learn to tune in, we can pick up emotions and feelings at a physiological level. The science behind these cues is called "somatic marker" theory. Our "gut instincts" allow our brains to make a call about a future action, based on what our body is telling us or has told us in the past. Tension in our shoulders

---

[23] "Our irrational emotional life." Susan Krauss Whitbourne. Ph.D. Jan. 25, 2014. Psychology Today.

[24] "Why we should care about emotions at work." Sue Langley blog. Langley Group. October 28, 2015.

or hands may be hinting at rising anger; while the desire to get up and move may indicate excitement.[25]

Maslow's Hierarchy of Needs Within the Organization

With respect to the hierarchy of needs, it is often instructive to consider what the benefits are that organizations (especially compassionate organizations) can and do deliver to their employees. Some of the key benefits that people derive by working in organizations include:

- A sense of belonging.
- Shared values and beliefs.
- Sense of purpose (their work has meaning) and accomplishment.
- A livelihood.
- Career mobility.

Compassionate organizations tend to place great emphasis on building a strong reputational brand through its informal culture that they apply in promoting their causes, ethics, and sense of purpose in terms of their contributions to the world they perform in. These caring and nurturing organizations also understand that it is in their best interest to understand how the hierarchy of needs can be best applied to the personal and professional development of each employee.

EMOTIONAL LABOR

Emotional labor is an employee's expression of organizationally desired emotions during interpersonal transactions at work. Think of it as acting the role of what our organization demands of us. One aspect of labor is emotional dissonance, or "**Faking it.**" Dissonance occurs when we have to show one emotion, but we feel another. One sure fire approach to take so as not to have to fake our behavior when we go to work is to find employment in an organization whose ethics and values match our own.

---

[25] "Why we should care about emotions at work." Sue Langley blog. Langley Group. October 28, 2015.

AFFECTIVE EVENTS THEORY

Under the Affective Events Theory, employees react emotionally to the things that happen to them at work. When people say "It's not personal, it's business" that is just not true. Everything we experience in the workplace or outside of it is personal to us. That is part of our human condition.

Our reactions to the events we experience play a big part in influencing our job performance and satisfaction. Work events trigger either positive or negative emotional reactions. Thus, it is critical for organizations that wish to optimize employee performance and thus productivity to begin to provide their people with the tools and training that is required to optimize their EQ.

Emotions are such a critical part of the at-work experience, that there is a growing field of research into reading emotions from facial expressions. Reference the research being conducted Dan Hill of Facial Expressions Research.

26

---

26 From Ethan Chazin's program: "Become Emotionally Intelligent for Relationship Success." 2016.

3. Diversity and Inclusion

When I was speaking to the HR Executive Leaders of the New Jersey Bankers Association at their annual conference last year I asked the audience: "Does your management team pass the EYEBALL test?"

What I meant was: "How can you hope to shape the future diversity and inclusiveness of the NJ banking industry?" The room was filled with folks who were as a whole entirely too white, too male, and too old to possess the correct mindset and frame of reference to offer meaningful workplace cultures to a diverse Millennial workforce.

Why does diversity matter to organizations?

It helps to acknowledge that, for as much diversity as organizations have achieved to date, white male dominance remains a persistent challenge despite the following:

- Many organizations have made progress in terms of more equitable pay and gender-balanced employment.
- There has been a huge influx of non-White professionals especially Asians and Latinos in the workforce.
- White males still remain a dominant force in the ranks of management.
- Aging Workforce.
- There is a huge difference between Surface-level and Deep-level diversity.
- For two decades, there has been an infusion of veterans in our American workforce.

> **According to the U.S. Census Bureau, the majority of people in the U.S will identify as people of color within the next 40 years. Statistics from the U.S. Dept. of Commerce show the *minority business community is growing at twice the rate of the general business population.*[27]**

A lack of true diversity is just one contributor to organizational imbalance. Another factor that creates organizational imbalance is the persistent gender imbalance that exists in far too many American organizations. Of the Fortune 500 top U.S. firms in 2013, only 4% of those companies had female CEOs. The gender imbalance (glass ceiling) is still firmly in place, and a major barrier preventing true organizational compassion.

Here's how organizations can overcome these built-in generations-long systemic challenges to achieving a diverse workplace that reflects the community it works in, and the composition of the clients it serves, partners/vendors it works with, and society at large:

- **You Can't Motivate People Equally**: people from the SAME ethnic background, possessing the SAME level of education and the SAME socioeconomic background possess DIFFERENT interests, values and ethics thus requiring different motivations.

- **Get to Know All of the People You Work With**: It is impossible to create an inclusive work environment until you know enough about your people to understand what it takes to make them FEEL included.

- **The U.S. Times Are Changing**: You only have to look at the 2010 Census (or see the outcomes of our next 2020 census as proof. By 2020, the #1 language spoken in American homes will be... (DRUM ROLL, please!) – Spanish! The number of Hispanics and Asians in this country is rising at a much faster rate than Caucasians. As further proof of the significance of a growing American diversity, Millennials (ages 18-24) who make up 90 million Americans and 3 out of every FOUR American works

---

[27] Forbes.com/sites/entrepreneursorganization/2013/12/04/3-diversity-strategies -to-help-companies-thrive.

will be more than 50% non-Caucasian by 2020 for the first time in U.S. history.

- **More and MORE Non-White Males**: Women, Asians, and Hispanics are entering the American workplace in greater ranks as they increase in our communities, and as our clients, partners, suppliers, vendors!

- **Interracial Marriages Are Blending Ethnicities**: Another factor driving the need for more diverse workplaces is the rise in interracial couples in American society. According to the 2010 U.S. Census, about 17% of new marriages and 20% of cohabitating relationships are interracial or interethnic. About one quarter of all Americans have a close relative in an interracial marriage.[28]

> "We become not a melting pot but a beautiful mosaic. Different people. Different beliefs. Different yearnings. Different hopes. Different dreams."
> - Jimmy Carter

Organizations that wish to build a global team must apply a global perspective, which requires a complete transformation in its Senior leadership team and Board of Directors to reflect the world these organizations compete in.

Recruiting in the five (5) generation American society includes recruiting matures, baby boomers, Generation Xers, Millennials and the teenage Generation Z segment of our population. Coaching/mentoring is an invaluable tool for organizations to leverage, to help bridge the generational divide between the generations.

So, what makes each of the five generations of American worker tick? How can compassionate organizations create customized recruiting, talent acquisition, onboarding and retention strategies that appeal to each segment specifically? By getting to know what motivates each group, what is important to them, what they value, and what they seek from the organizations they wish to commit to.

1. The Matures

---

[28] "Interracial love is saving America." Sheryll Cashin. New York Times. June 4, 2017.

Matures, aka the "First" Generation, were born before 1945. At 30 million people, they comprise 10% of workforce, and were influenced by the Military, and are the most affluent group. Matures spent their formative years practicing "Delayed Gratification." They spent their lives adhering to the principle of work first, seek pleasure later.

2. Baby Boomers

Were born between 1945 and 1964. They represent an amazing mix of individual and collective *GREATNESS* by epitomizing both Idealism and Creativity coupled with a *NARCISSISTIC* attitude as the "ME" Generation. At 80 million people, they are the most influential group. Boomers are workaholics, and the spent their professional careers defining their work ethic by the amount of time they worked, and length of tenure at their employers.

Boomers place great value in being a team member, and cherish strong contributors to the teams they serve on. Approximately 10,000 Boomers a day are leaving the workforce, which is one of the single greatest and most influential trends in the American economy. Their code of conduct was built on honoring trust, loyalty, and personal responsibility. Boomers came of age distrusting authority.

3. Generation X

I am proud to admit that I one of the 45 million Generation Xers. We were born between 1964 and 1980, spent our teenage years with AIDS and MTV and became the "Prove it to me" Generation. We are the generational "bridge" between the Boomers and the Millennials. We are loyal to people, NOT organizations. We were forced to live through two great Recessions in 1990 and 2007. We spent our careers moving from job-to-job in a manner unknown to our predecessors. Our generational mantra can be defined as: "Carpe Diem - Seize the day!" Above all else, we value flexibility, life options, and achieving job satisfaction.

4. The Millennials / Generation Y

Next up…Millennials, those born between 1980 and 2000. 53 million people representing $172B in aggregate spending power. Millennials seek instant gratification, and desire quick feedback. They are extremely busy outside of work, and can be best rewarded with time to spend in their outside interests to maximize work-life balance.

They are focused on paying off their student loans, and want/expect paid leave from their ideal employer. Their quality of life at work is more valuable to them than pay. Grew up in prosperous times and therefore have high career and professional expectations. Millennials seek meaning in their work, and their career goals are most often aligned with becoming rich (81%) and famous (51%).

5. Generation Z / The "I" Generation (as in...iPhone, iPad, iTunes)

Finally, we come to the 'Post-Millennials'. These young professionals are comfortable with technology and are social media savvy experts. They came of age during "September 11th" and the Great Recession, so they are understandably collectively insecure and unsettled.

They value security/stability, over a sense of purpose and calling. They are much more like Boomers and Matures than they are Millennials. They report their top must-haves as health insurance (70%) competitive salary (63%), and a boss that I respect (61%). 67% are willing to relocate for work/a career. Lastly, Generation Z is: "Innovative, entrepreneurial, highly conscious of their futures and the challenges they face." - *Patrick Cooper*

> **"Organizations which excel at leveraging diversity (including the hiring and advancement of women and non-white men into senior management jobs, and providing a climate conducive to contributions from people of diverse backgrounds) will experience better financial performance in the long run than organizations which are not effective in managing diversity."**
> **- Equalitymagazine.com**

Before your organization goes down the path to meaningful diversity ask yourself: "Do I truly have the support, buy in, and long-term commitment of my management team?" If YES, proceed. If NO, stop!

Diversity must be built into your organization's culture. For starters, gauge the surface level diversity in your organization. Walk around. Does your workplace look like the rest of your industry? Your community? The world?

Diversity is not synonymous with filling quotas. It's so much more than finding the right balance between age, gender, and ethnicity. True organizational diversity takes a 'Global Village' view by embracing divergent employee backgrounds, beliefs, values, lifestyles, military service, upbringing, etc.

Sometimes, organizations have no choice but to be led down the Diversity and Inclusion path only after significant social and legal pressures have been forced upon them. Look no farther than the financial services industry for what can happen when organizations fail to diversify.

"Businesses started caring a lot more about diversity after a series of high-profile lawsuits rocked the financial industry. In the late 1990s and early 2000s, Morgan Stanley shelled out $54 million—and Smith Barney and Merrill Lynch more than $100 million each—to settle sex discrimination claims. In 2007, Morgan was back at it, facing a new class action lawsuit, which cost the company $46 million. In 2013, Bank of America Merrill Lynch settled a race discrimination suit for $160 million. Cases like these brought Merrill's total 15-year payout to nearly *half a billion* dollars."[29] Ouch!

How does your organization embrace differences? Are you prepared to take your organization from a mindset of merely tolerating diversity to advocating for a diverse workplace? After I gave a talk on Diversity & Inclusion to a group of HR executives of the NJ Bankers Association, a Senior-level HR executive of a predominantly African American bank in Newark, NJ approached me.

She asked if we could meet to explore strategies to build a diverse workforce that more closely mirrored the changing population of Newark, NJ and their business banking customers. After we met, I provided her with a list of immediate strategies the bank should implement, in order to achieve immediate and meaningful diversity. I then waited for her decision whether or not we would be proceeding. And I waited, and waited. In speaking to employees of the bank since then, I understand that no initiatives have been undertaken. Clearly, she either lacked the authority, personal commitment, or senior-level buy in to proceed.

The benefits your organization derives from achieving true diversity and inclusion extend far beyond legal compliance to include:

---

[29] https://hbr.org/2016/07/why-diversity-programs-fail.

- More effectively connecting with your customers;
- Motivating your employees;
- Fostering greater innovation and creativity since people from different backgrounds challenge each other and having people from different backgrounds fosters a constantly evolving culture;
- Becoming a preferred employer, which makes your job easier;
- Increase your recruiting pool; and
- The ability to conduct business in more markets across cultural boundaries.

Research supports the need for diversity in your workplace. Why? A VillageLife.com survey conducted by *Melissa Lauber* and whose findings were reported in the federal Glass Ceiling Commission found that diversity has a positive impact on organization bottom lines. Thus, compassionate organizations that achieve meaningful diversity positively impact their financial performance.

A study conducted by Covenant Investment Management rated the performance of the organizations listed on the Standard & Poor 500 on a series of factors relating to the hiring and advancement of women and nonwhites.

The study concluded that the annual return of the 100 companies with the LOWEST in equal employment rankings averaged 7.9%, compared to an aggregate performance level of 18.3% for the 100 companies that rated HIGHEST in equal employment.

Three other meaningful studies that concluded a positive causal relationship between the positive impact of diversity on compassionate organization's financial performance:

1. Frank Dobbin (Harvard University) and Alexandra Kalev analyzed diversity in hundreds of U.S. companies over 3 decades. Their findings were striking:

"In analyzing three decades' worth of data from more than 800 U.S. firms and interviewing hundreds of line managers and executives at length, we've seen that companies get better results when they ease up on the control tactics. It's more effective to engage managers in solving the problem, increase their on-the-job contact with female and minority workers, and promote social accountability—the desire to look fair-minded. That's why interventions such as targeted college recruitment, mentoring programs, self-managed teams, and task forces have boosted diversity in businesses. Some of the most effective solutions aren't even designed with diversity in mind." [30]

2. In a McKinsey study entitled: "Diversity Matters" that was conducted by Vivian Hunt, Dennis Layton, Sara Prince were also noteworthy in the positive correlation between diversity and organizational financial performance:

"Our latest research finds that companies in the top quartile for gender or racial and ethnic diversity are more likely to have financial returns above their national industry medians. Companies in the bottom quartile in these dimensions are statistically less likely to achieve above-average returns. And diversity is probably a competitive differentiator that shifts market share toward more diverse companies over time." [31]

3. The positive impact on an organization's ability to compete through management's efforts to achieve diversity, in terms of the company's stock price valuation.

"This study's premise is that firms that can lower their costs and enhance their differentiation through the effective management of their human resources have a competitive advantage. Using data from 1986 through 1992, we examined the impact that announcements of U.S. Department of Labor awards for exemplary affirmative action programs had upon the stock returns of winning corporations and the effect that announcements of damage awards from the settlement of discrimination lawsuits had on the stock returns of corporations. The results suggest that announcements of awards may be associated with competitive advantage and that discrimination-related announcements may be associated with inability to achieve such advantage." [32]

According to the Society of Human Resource Management: "**Diversity is marketable!**" Diversity can be the catalyst you need, to achieve a better ROI

---

[30] https://hbr.org/2016/01/diversity-policies-dont-help-women-or-minorities-and-they-make-white-men-feel-threatened.

[31] www.mckinsey.com/business-functions/organization/our-insights/why-diversity-matters.

[32] www.researchgate.net/publication/245723703_Competitiveness_Through_Management_of_Diversity_Effects_of_Stock_Price_Valuation.

from your people's performance. Consider the following when assessing the need for your organization to embrace greater Diversity & Inclusion:

- Minorities are a majority in *6 of the 8* largest U.S. cities;
- Women and minorities show greater interest in employers that customize their recruiting efforts to them.
- Blacks, Hispanics and Asians combined for more than *$870 billion* in purchases; and
- Women are the primary investors in *more than half* of all U.S. households.

What Does "Inclusion" Mean in Organizations

So far, I have spoken about Diversity, but how can organizations create an inclusive environment that make their people feel welcome, and part of something greater than themselves? After all, through Inclusion you build employee trust which in turn leads to loyalty, a heightened level of commitment and engagement.

Inclusion begins BEFORE the employee's first day when you send them their acceptance letter. Typically, organizations use that first communication as a means of laying out the terms of their employment. They set forth the rules, regulations, and lots of "You Musts!" right out of the gate.

Instead, consider that first moment as a chance to build a sense of "Wow!" by the employee. Why not email the new hire a "Hello, Welcome to Our Team" video message from the CEO/Executive Director?

Mail them a gift basket with goodies including company-branded merchandise and other things for them and their families (if applicable). Be sure to include a welcome letter reiterating your organization's Vision, Mission, values and employees come first creed/message. When they arrive at their office for the first day, bring them to their office/cubicle which should already be set up with their equipment, employee ID, and other relevant access to online systems, paperwork. Maybe consider creating a temporary access to your employee Intranet. Balloons, welcome mugs, team members blowing kazoos, are all really nice touches. Schedule face time with their Department Head, have an Ambassador" from your Senior Management Team greet them, and give them the "walk around tour."

Their boss should take them to lunch, explain the Team and organization's Vision, Mission, goals, and values. Thus, you need to train your leaders how to "include" new members. Consider having new hires get scheduled for an onboarding orientation, provide access to resources such as memberships in your industry's trade Associations. Let them know about any of your organization's "affinity" groups such as NextGen future Leaders, the Latinas in Information Science & Technology group, your company's softball Team.

Making employees feel included can be achieved through many creative ways, such as idea solicitation programs, signing them up to your coaching and mentoring program, including them in reward and recognition initiatives, and including them in Teams at an early stage of their tenure with you. Once you have engaged and included employees, why not make employee Brand Ambassador video testimonials that you can use in your organization's recruiting and marketing efforts, as "case studies" showing how happy your people are?

Simply stated, "Inclusion" is the collective acts your organization goes through to make each and every person (full-time employee, temporary employee/contract worker/freelancer) feel that they are a welcome addition to, and part of, your organization.

Benefits Organizations Gain from Embracing D&I

The benefits of workplace diversity are significant. Following is a starting point you can use to "sell" the importance of developing a campaign in your place of business to your Management extend far beyond legal compliance to include:

- Possessing a diverse workforce will enable your organization to more effectively connecting with customers;
- Having a more diverse workforce is an empowering organizational tool to motivate your employees;
- Diversity fosters greater innovation and creativity, as people from different backgrounds challenge each other and having people from different backgrounds fosters a constantly evolving culture;
- Enables your organization to become a preferred employer, which makes YOUR talent acquisition job MUCH easier;

- Gives you a MUCH larger recruiting pool to source talented employees from;
- The ability to conduct business in more markets across cultural boundaries;
- Facilitate a more agile learning culture;

How Diversity Initiatives Can Backfire.

Organizations wishing to become more compassionate by developing diversity and inclusion need to be careful, especially when it comes to failing to fully implement programs because half measures without long-term commitments can backfire.

"A study of 700+ U.S. companies found that implementing diversity training programs has little positive effect and may even *decrease* representation of black women. Most people assume that diversity policies make companies fairer for women and minorities, though the data suggest otherwise. Even when there is clear evidence of discrimination at a company, the presence of a diversity policy leads people to discount claims of unfair treatment.

In previous research, we've found that this is especially true for members of dominant groups and those who tend to believe that the system is generally fair. In another set of experiments, we found that diversity initiatives also seem to do little to convince minorities that companies will treat them more fairly." [33] - **Tessa Dover, Cheryl Kaiser, Brenda Major**

---

[33] https://hbr.org/2016/01/diversity-policies-dont-help-women-or-minorities-and-they-make-white-men-feel-threatened.

Recruit Superheroes.

One extremely effective strategy that compassionate organizations have implemented in order to achieve meaningful diversity and inclusion is to avoid hiring based on specific pedigree such as schools attended, GPA, field of study. Instead, seek out the attributes of top performers as a way to recruit superheroes into your organization.

Specific attributes to hire for when you recruit Superheroes include:

- Risk-takers.
- Thrive in chaos.
- Work independently.
- Self-motivated.
- Respond well to change.
- Leaders.
- Strong relationship-builders.
- Great teammates.
- Problem-solvers/Critical thinkers.

Which of these attributes does your organization specifically recruit for?

Begin by asking your Managers, Department Heads, and Business Unit leaders: **"What do all high performers in our company - across all positions - have in common?"** [34]

Embed Diversity & Inclusion in ALL Your Hiring Efforts.

Discuss your diversity strategies in all of your company marketing promotional materials, job postings, and emphasize your organization's vision, mission, values, and story. MAKE DIVERSITY PART OF YOUR BRAND! Diversity is so critically important to an organization's success that in May, 2017 Apple hired **Denise Young Smith**, who headed its Global Human Resources program, as its first ever Vice President of Diversity and Inclusion.

---

[34] Workforce.com/articles/21787-the-big-lie-of-hiring-for-cultural-fit.

Your Diversity Action Plan.

MAKE DIVERSITY WORK FOR YOU. You can build an amazingly powerful diversity plan by following this checklist of best practices. Review your talent acquisition plan with a renewed focus on where you have sourced talent from in the past (geographic focus) to find new talent. Following is a comprehensive list of quick hit strategies your organization can embrace in order to develop a successful diversity program:

- Pay particular attention to helping your minority/underrepresented employees on-board by acclimating them quickly into your organization's culture.
- Expand your reach into more diverse talent pools, by leveraging local community organizations such as incubators, Tech MeetUps, Marketing Executive Networking Group, Finance Executive Networking Group, Rotary, Toastmasters, BNI, LeTip, etc.
- Include Diversity websites in your online recruiting efforts.
- Emulate the best practices of organizations that have already achieved success in your industry. In this case, it is acceptable to take a "Follow the leader" approach. I am suggesting that you add Recruiting as a formal function to your organization's competitive intelligence gathering efforts.
- Create well thought out Equal Opportunity Employment policy following guidelines set forth by the Equal Employment Opportunity Commission.
  The Goal: "meritorious (performance-based) hiring practice that is…age, race, gender, and minority NEUTRAL."
- DIVERSITY training. Teach your Human Resources and Senior Management teams first, and then apply an organization-wide "trickle down" approach to train middle management, line managers, and Supervisors!
- Learn from past mistakes! Conduct EXIT interviews to get to the heart of why these Superheroes are leaving the organization.
- Diversity's driven "*top-down*" but felt from the "*bottom-up*." Plant the seed to your organizations' future diversity growth, by bringing in a diverse group of interns. Provide scholarships, fellowships, and co-op work experience to help minorities in

college who you want to aggressively recruit before they graduate and find employment elsewhere.

- Add a Diversity Policy statement to your annual strategic plan.
- Include *diversity*-oriented questions in your employee surveys.
- Set up business resource **'affinity' groups** within your organization. Examples of affinity groups include African-Americans, Young professionals (NextGen Leaders), Hispanics (LISTA), GLBT networks, etc.
- Track your retention success rates across groups and by recruiting sources. Whatever is working best for you, keep up with it. Whatever isn't, cut that from your recruiting program. Keep revisiting, as recruiting is an iterative, 365-day a year endeavor.
- Take a stance on diversity-related public policy issues. For example, Microsoft supported a Washington state gay rights bill.
- **YOU** have to be the ***Change Agent*** that changes the behaviors of your hiring managers. Ask people in positions of power within your organization: "***What/how do you think about 'differences here?'***" Find Champion leaders within your organization who are already embracing Diversity in their hiring/team-building initiatives in their own business Units/areas. Employ them as "Diversity coaches" to apply their best practices across your organization.
- Use assessment tools to gauge your people's "***intra* AND *inter* cultural sensitivity.**"
- Embrace culturally-specific networking strategies, such as targeting groups that your organization has typically not actively recruited in the past or are under-represented in your employee ranks.
- Hold Managers accountable for diversity goals by making diversity part of your annual performance review process.
- Organizations that assign responsibility for diversity achieve better results from diversity training, evaluations, and mentoring programs.
- Support flexible work arrangements, on-site child daycare, job sharing, and other job satisfaction programs.

Go Get It Done!

Following is a checklist of immediately actionable steps that you can take, in order to achieve meaningful diversity and inclusion within your organization.

- Offer a formal **coaching/mentoring** program to employees across, up, and down the organization. Match new employee hires with your firm's most trusted and respected Brand Ambassadors as part of your Coaching & Mentoring program.
- Create a full-time *Diversity Officer* position, and a cross-functional *Diversity Team* led by your Diversity Officer, tasked with achieving your firm's annual diversity/inclusion goals.
- **Your CEO must LEAD BY EXAMPLE**. YOU need THEM to set the tone by walking the walk of importance for diversity to be universally embraced and accepted within your organization.
- Set quotas in your recruiting strategy. Yes, I said the "Q" word. Quotas. These are quantifiable targets to achieve D&I staffing levels that overcome/rectify your past organizational shortcomings.
- Provide opportunities for rising stars/top performers to receive education and professional development. Review your organization's process for identifying who rising stars are and where they come from.
- Get Management's commitment to a formal Diversity program "IN WRITING". This will include an annual budget, key deliverables to be achieved as goals, a "Champion" to own the program (ideally your D&I officer/Team. Allocate resources (a working budget) that cannot be "taken away" at the discretion of Senior Management. Institute a 5-year "no touch" policy so the budget is safeguarded for that period of time.
- Develop a Diversity Policy Statement that is communicated within the organization and make it a critical selling point in all of your recruiting efforts. Go so far as to place it on the Careers area of your website, and all of your job descriptions
- Document your organization's Vision, Mission, Values, and History everywhere which includes within your organization, and in your external marketing efforts.

- Identify your Ideal Employee Attributes and your most successful Recruiting sources/strategies.
- Conduct an assessment across your organization to determine the current state of your diversity and inclusion program. Ask yourself what is working/not working. Which Divisions/Units/offices are really embracing D&I. Which are woefully underperforming. Make changes on an "as-needed" basis all year long.
- List of specific actions you will undertake to achieve and maintain Diversity (see: "**Get it done.**")
- Build an archive of Employee Testimonials. These are positive employee statements about how your organization actively encourages them to achieve their full potential. Your happy employees are truly the "face" of a successful D&I program.
- Communicate your Diversity Plan to ALL of your employees.
- Employee Referral Program: Have your top talent refer people like themselves who possess the same super hero skills and come from underrepresented employee groups.

Define your organization's current and future hiring goals using *Gender and Ethnicity* driven targets.

For example:

YEAR	2010	2016	2020	Goal/Target
Male	75%	65%	55%	â 20%
Female	25%	35%	45%	á 20%
Black	5%	8%	10%	á 5%
Hispanic	5%	7%	10%	á 5%
Asian	8%	13%	15%	á 7%
White	82%	72%	65%	â 17%

"We focus on two things when hiring. First, find the best people you can in the world. And second, let them do their own work. Just get out of their way."
- Matt Mullenweg, Automattic, Inc. Serial Entrepreneur

Define your organization's current and desired hiring goals by <u>Functional Area</u>. (Customer Care, HR, R&D, etc.)

Customer Svc.	2010	2016	2020	HR	2010	2016	2020	R&D	2010	2016	2020
Male	30%	40%	50%	Male	15%	25%	35%	Male	100%	95%	90%
Female	70%	60%	50%	Female	85%	75%	65%	Female	0%	5%	10%
Black	10%	15%	20%	Black	5%	10%	15%	Black	0%	5%	5%
Hispanic	15%	20%	25%	Hispanic	10%	15%	20%	Hispanic	0%	0%	5%
Asian	5%	10%	15%	Asian	5%	5%	10%	Asian	25%	40%	50%
White	70%	55%	40%	White	80%	70%	55%	White	75%	55%	40%

Michael Gavin's TED talk "Why cultural diversity matters."

Gavin, Associate Professor of human dimensions of natural resources researches biological diversity, and discusses the importance that history, language and tradition have in the preservation of culture. He claims that we need a diverse set of skills in order to cope with the wicked uncertainties of today.

Measures to Defend Your Organization

As a way of building a truly diverse workforce, I often coach organizations to come to grips with their patterns of discriminatory behavior. Organizations get into trouble when they find themselves: "*Noting of a difference between things; often referred to making judgments about individuals based on stereotypes regarding their demographic group.*"

Discrimination can be leveraged at job seekers, candidates, and existing employees on the following basis: Age, Gender, Race, Sexual Orientation/ Gender Identity, Politics, Cultural Identity, Religion and their intellectual abilities. The challenge organizations face is, not all of these are obvious. There are many grey areas that pose as potential quagmires that you can and likely have fallen into often without knowing.

Check out the TED talk by *Andres Tapia* on the idea of **upside down diversity** and how so much of what we THINK we know about the world is backwards.

To help organizations minimize potential damaging (and ILLEGAL) patterns of discriminatory behavior, it helps to gain a clear understanding/preach:

- (Discriminatory) behavior is a true reflection of the organization's culture, and by extension its Founder(s) and Senior Management / leadership team.
- You need to adopt an absolute "Zero Tolerance" policy.
- Senior Management sets the tone for the degree of discrimination that is tolerated in your workplace.
- HR is responsible for serving as your organization's guardian/ defender of employee rights and gatekeeper that keeps discriminatory behavior OUT.
- Requires defined policies and procedures. You can't defend what is not explicitly defined in your organization's policies and procedures. Create an organizational CREDO/MANIFESTO.
- Address/state your D&I mission in your employee orientation handbook, new hire on-boarding initiatives, and your employee training and professional development programs.

4. Self-Managed Teams

A Brief History of Self-Managed Teams

The idea of self-managed teams of workers getting together or working remotely to achieve shared goals without Management's interference has been around for a very long time.

The American workplace has evolved from an industrial to post-Industrial workforce driven by service, software, technology, and global competition. With the internet, social media, the sharing economy, gig "freelance" workplace and a majority of Millennials overtaking Boomers and Generation Xers, the compassionate organization is moving to a "**Participation**" based-approach to work.

In his TED talk entitled: "The Emerging Work World in the Participation Age," **Chuck Blakeman** rightly points out that we are now living at the intersection of fundamentally opposed work world views. On one side stands the 19th - 20th Century Industrial world. On the other is the Participation Age. On the industrial side, Managers still make most if not all organizational decisions, while employees function as merely extensions of machines and thus a cost to be contained. This outdated world collides painfully with the evolving 21st Century Millennial-driven Participation Age. In this new world order, employees want/need to have MEANING at work, not just seek profits. In short, they want to take ownership of their work. [35]

The concept of self-managed teams in the American workplace dates back to the 1960s. At that time, an early experiment by General Foods Corporation to consider deploying self-managed teams for its Gaines dog-food production line proved the concept could be applied even as its Senior Management expected the project to fail.

---

[35] www.youtube.com/watch?v=ewA2BqbWhUQ. Chuck Blakeman. TEDx Mile High. July 16, 2014.

> Today, approximately 80% of the companies in the
> Fortune 1000 and 81% of manufacturing companies
> leverage some form of self-managed employee teams.

A New Organizational Structure called Holacracy

Holacracy was a term phrased by Arthur Koestler in his book: "The Ghost in the Machine" to define such worker-driven self-directed teams. Other terms used to define self-managed teams include: worker self-management, self-managed workplaces, self-directed employees, peer-to-peer training, and labor-managed firms.

What does holacracy sounds like? Here's Tony Hsieh, CEO of Zappos to explain: "So we're trying to figure out how to structure Zappos more like a city, and less like a bureaucratic corporation. In a city, people and businesses are self-organizing. We're trying to do the same thing by switching from a normal hierarchical structure to a system called Holacracy, which enables employees to act more like entrepreneurs and self-direct their work instead of reporting to a manager who tells them what to do." [36]

Holacracy offers a system for employee self-management in organizations. Holacracy replaces the traditional command-control management hierarchy with a new peer-to-peer "operating system" that increases transparency, accountability, and organizational agility. By openly stating the rules to self-management and creating the structure needed for self-managed Teams, Holacracy allows businesses to distribute authority up-down, and across the organization, empowering all employees to take a leadership role and make meaningful decisions.[37]

What is a Self-Managed Work Team?

Teams form organically without management intrusion around clearly defined objectives. Employees enter willingly into short-term team circles to set their collective desired results and define the processes required to achieve those short/long-term goals. Self-managed teams are basically left to run themselves, with guidance provided by an external leader on an "as-needed"

---

[36] www.holacracy.org.
[37] www.holacracy.org.

basis. The external leader role is often considered much more complicated than a traditional manager, as the external leader often balances leading multiple teams thus bouncing from team to team.

Employees in these self-directed teams take complete ownership of their work (and decision-making authority) as well as the results (and profits) they achieve. Employees form teams with the autonomy to make their own decisions and structure their work without managerial involvement, in order to work on specific projects as opportunities and challenges present themselves.

These teams tend to have very well-defined job functions and are responsible for managing and monitoring their own performance. They also possess an external leader who takes the place of a traditional manager. These leaders must walk a fine line between being seen by their Senior Management as too relaxed with their teams, and the teams they manage who may see them as interfering.

Why Self-Managed Teams Are So Powerful.

More and more Millennial workers are demanding the option of managing their own work and taking ownership of what they work on, how they approach their work, the responsibility of achieving shared goals in a team-driven environment with minimal external interference. This younger generation of professionals want to obtain meaning from their work, and they strive to have an impact and take on work that matters while performing that work autonomously.

Boomers who came into power in the 1980s are being forced to react to and accommodate Millennial employee expectations to contribute in meaningful ways to the organizations they join.

Embracing self-managed work teams is often the fastest path to achieving lasting employee engagement, a term that is currently in vogue in many business and consulting circles.

Examples Abound.

One company that has achieved competitive advantage and market leader status by leveraging self-managed teams is Morningstar, a California-based tomato processor. "The Morning Star Company was built on a foundational philosophy of Self-Management. We envision an organization of self-managing professionals who initiate communication and coordination of their activities with fellow colleagues, customers, suppliers and fellow industry participants, absent directives from others.

For colleagues to find joy and excitement utilizing their unique talents and to weave those talents into activities which complement and strengthen fellow colleagues' activities. And for colleagues to take personal responsibility and hold themselves accountable for achieving our Mission." [38]

Other firms that have successfully embraced self-managed teams include: WL Gore, Zappos, Cap Management, Realize, Sounds True, 37 Signals, The Container Store, and Timberland. At WL Gore, the Company's stated culture as reflected by Bill Gore, its Founder revolves around employee collaboration and engagement:

> *Our Culture. Innovation, integrity and teamwork drive our business every day.*
>
> I dreamed of an enterprise with great opportunity for all who would join in it, a virile organization that would foster self-fulfillment and which would multiply the capabilities of the individuals comprising it beyond their mere sum. (Bill Gore, 1961.) At Gore's workplaces around the globe, there's a buzz in the air — an excitement for the work Gore does and the work each Associate brings to the enterprise. [39]
>
> It starts with that word, "Associate." We're more than employees; we're trusted stewards of our business. Each of us makes commitments that help drive the business, and we work together in our lattice communications structure. In this structure, we collaborate and build connections without the constraints of traditional chains of command — giving us the freedom to encourage and support each other's growth and development. It's an environment in which highly motivated people thrive and where we are

---

[38] http://morningstarco.com/index.cgi?Page=Self-Management.
[39] www.gore.com/about/culture.

able to bring our unique talents and diverse perspectives to problem-solve and collectively get our work done.[40]

John Mackey, CEO of Whole Foods has identified part of the company's competitive advantage as having built a culture of self-managed teams. In each store, the decentralized approach relies upon 8-10 self-managed teams that are responsible for the operations of the store. They make all decisions including merchandising, compensation, etc. and employees are rewarded through team-based gain-sharing, as opposed to personal performance. 92% of Whole Foods stock options go to non-executive employees. Compare that to other corporations, where 75% of options go to their TOP 5 EXECUTIVES.[41]

Potential Drawbacks to Implementation.

There are several drawbacks to implementing worker-driven teams. A major barrier to implementation is the built-in inefficiency that arises when you avoid traditional organizational hierarchy and "chain of command."

There are fewer paths to career advancement in organizations with self-managed teams. This is true because organizations are leaner as they have removed many layers of management. Decades of organizational downsizing in the middle management ranks has led to leaner organizations, which tends to limit vertical moves within the organization. Also, if you work in such self-managed culture and wish to move to a more traditional firm culture, it is often challenging to effectively describe your work performance and contributions in the non-traditional self-managed team environment.

Overly cohesive teams that tend to align strongly with the group's values can lead to "Groupthink" in which members fail to question the ideas, values and decisions reached by the team. Independent thought is put aside in the quest to achieve conformity.

Implementing a change in culture to take advantage of employee self-managed teams becomes difficult when you have to decide to remove layers of management. Where do you re-assign those managers? Another challenge is how you get management staff to (willingly) fire themselves?

---

[40] www.gore.com/about/culture

[41] Joseph Weiss. "Business Ethics: A stakeholder and Issues Management approach." Pg. 238.

A Path to Implement Self-Managed Teams.

There are eight (8) steps that are required to create an organizational culture of self-managed teams:

1. Form a team around a set of objectives.
2. Define your desired results of achieving these goals.
3. Identify all of the processes needed to obtain your desired results.
4. Set metrics for the steps in the process.
5. Determine the pay based on achieving these results.
6. Decide what happens if the metrics are not met and how to move team members along if they are not contributing.
7. Obtain Leadership approval to proceed.
8. Implement the team.

Teams, Generally Speaking...

In today's ultra-competitive world, teams are EVERYWHERE. Building engaged and well-functioning teams can serve as the greatest competitive advantage an organization leverages in democratizing decision-making, empowering its people, and unleashing their untapped potential.

Watch **Barry Schwartz's** TED talk: *"The Way We Think About Work is Broken."* He notes that we don't work merely to make a living and for material rewards. In fact, he points out that this is a bad reason to explain the motivation for why we work. He also states that for an overwhelming majority of the global workforce the work they do has none of the motivating characteristics of what gets us up every day to get to work. Their work is monotonous, and they do it only for pay. [42]

Ever hear of the "**Marshmallow Problem**" on using marshmallows to build a tower as a means of getting people to work together?

Take a look at the TED talk by **Tom Wujek**: "Build a Tower, Build a Team" for insights into how to build powerful teams that work productively together. I use this as an "ice breaker" exercise to get my college students and my clients to begin to work in more collaborative and results-focused Teams.

---

[42] Barry Schwartz: "Why do we work," TED talk. Vancouver, BC. March, 2014.

Work Groups Differ from Work Teams.

There is a very important distinction to be made between GROUPS and TEAMS.

The term "work groups" is often used inter-changeably with 'teams," when in fact groups and teams operate differently. Here's a list of work group characteristics that distinguish groups from teams:

- Group members interact primarily to share information and make decisions. There is no requirement to forge stronger interpersonal relationships. The focus is the work required to be competed.
- The Group's performance is just a collection of each's personal contributions. People don't work together, there's minimal "esprit-d-corp" or sense of being "in it together." In groups...I do my work, you do yours.
- In work teams, members coordinate their efforts and work together to accomplish goals with a view towards establishing greater trust and familiarity which can be leveraged as members work together on future efforts.

Types of Teams You Can Create.

There are five types of team that can be formed based on the people involved, tasks to be completed and the degree of working together that is required. They are:

1. **Problem-Solving**: 5-12 employees get together a few hours each week to discuss ways to improve things.
2. **Self-Managed**: Teams that solve problems AND implement solutions and are responsible for outcomes.
3. **Cross-Functional:** Members from different areas at the same level come together to accomplish specific tasks.
4. **Virtual Teams**: Dispersed members use technology to maintain contact. They collaborate online, use videoconferencing services like Skype and may or may not ever come into physical contact with each other.

5. **Multi-Team Systems:** Collections of 2 or more interdependent teams that share a goal. Imagine R&D teams that work on the thousands of component systems that comprise a 747 airliner.

In **Greg Brockman's** article "Six Secrets for Building a Super Team" [43] he shares his top six recruiting strategies for building an amazing team:

1. Only hire people who make others want to be around them.
2. Each new hire should increase the team's quality.
3. Never make a hire simply to fill an immediate need.
4. Take the time (make the effort) to integrate new team members.
5. Be willing to let people go, but hate doing it.
6. Everyone gets to veto a new team addition.

Building strong teams begins with trust. You need the right mix of personalities, according to **Peggy Drexler**. As an example, think back to the 2016 U.S. women's Olympic soccer team.

Team Member Diversity is Key.

- A major research study concluded that demographic diversity is unrelated to overall team performance, and race and gender based diversity are negatively tied to performance.[44]
- Leadership can improve the performance of diverse teams.
- Keeping teams small is the key to improving the group's overall effectiveness.
- High performing groups contain people who prefer to work in teams.

Team Processes for Optimal Performance.

Following are key aspects of Teams that need to be actively managed in order to achieve optimal performance:

---

[43] https://gigaom.com/2012/04/28/6-secrets-for-building-a-super-team.

[44] "Getting Specific about Demographic Diversity Variable and Team Performance Relationships: A Meta-Analysis." Suzanne T. Bell Anton J. Villado Marc A. Lukasik Larisa Belau Andrea L. Briggs. Journal of Management.

- **Common plan and purpose**: A clear sense of what needs to be done and how that is shared by all members.
- **Specific goals**: Specific, measurable, and realistic performance goals that team members all "buy into" and make a commitment to achieving.
- **Team efficacy**: effective teams believe they can succeed.

- **Mental models**: mental representations of the key elements in the team's environment that members share.
- **Conflict levels**: Conflict isn't always bad. In fact, conflict, when effectively managed leads to increased idea generation, stronger team member relationship building and a greater degree of buy-in on the decisions reached from a majority of members.

Team Players CAN be Made

- Select people that can deliver on their individual roles.
- Provide training to build team skills (communication, negotiation, conflict resolution.)
- Foster a strong TEAM dynamic (we're in it together.)
- Reward cooperative behavior.

Speaking of building great teams...**remember the original US Men's Basketball Olympic Dream Team**? They represented the epitome of the world's (NBA's) best players putting aside personal egos to be able to be a part of a Team destined for greatness.

When No one (and EVERYONE) is the Boss

A new way to structure teams for unleashing people's untapped full potential entails removing the Manager role.

Times When Teamwork May NOT Be the Answer:

- Working together requires a time and resource investment.
- The benefits don't always exceed the costs associated.
- Does the work REQUIRE being performed in a Team, or will all members in the Team BENEFIT from the collective effort?

- Can the work be done better with more than one worker? Or is there a law of diminishing returns involved when you add members?
- Are the members of the group inter-dependent or can they work independently?
- Does the work create a common purpose or set of goals for group members?

Building Successful Global Teams.

In today's global economy, organizations are looking to expand their business by seeking out new markets. This places pressure on Senior Management to build Teams that are located all over the world, which in turn demands the ability to lead a virtual dispersed workforce.

Global Teams Reduce Time to Market – Follow the Sun

In the race for significant Time to Market gains, many organizations are re-thinking how they work, globally, to give themselves a competitive advantage. This often includes a "follow the sun" approach to collaborative, distributed design. In a "follow the sun" model, tasks are handed off at given points of time between a number of geographically distributed work sites that are many time zones apart. This kind of workflow is implemented in order to reduce overall project duration and increase relative effectiveness. Thus, the work is "following the sun" and never actually stops. [45]

In my work consulting with organizations to build global workplaces, I have developed a list of best practices that you can apply.

1. **Apply standard recruiting guidelines**: You should be able to apply "best practices" globally by creating a profile of your desired employee who matches your ideal employee characteristics to best deliver your organization's Corporate vision and mission statements and that shares your organization's corporate culture ethics and values. You do this while still taking into consideration the Superhero employee qualities specific to local regional/country distinctions.

---

[45] Christian Reilly, CTO Citrix LinkedIn blog. "Citrix HDI Ready Pi: At the heart of the next generation of Extreme Collaboration. April 25, 2017.

2. Apply **Coaching and mentoring programs** for team-building success, to embrace cultural and ethnic differences and similarities.

Coaching & Mentoring Program Goals

- Identify candidates using a clearly-defined set of criteria.
- Reduce turnover rates.
- Communicate the requirements throughout your organization.
- Hold a kick-off meeting for each session conducted.

Introduction

Promising employees with extremely significant performance potential require much more than simply industry expertise to become effective leaders. They also need to develop effective leadership skills that can be delivered through a well-developed mentoring/coaching program.

During each session's kick-off meeting, you need to communicate to the participants the company's vision, mission, short and long-term (3-5 year) strategic objectives.

Participant Selection Process

You need to solicit feedback from Managers on their star performers to be participated in the program committee (executive committee or senior management team). Set guidelines limiting the number of participants (such as one employee per department) per session. The goal is to always be selective in the nominating process, to weed out below average candidates through such screening criteria (ex. an interview or application process.)

Matching Process

The "pairing" process between program mentor and participant needs to have clearly defined procedures/criteria to ensure a greater likelihood of success in the pairing process:

- Senior and junior-level
- Different departments to avoid intra-departmental politics
- Personality type matching - Conduct an assessment of each mentor and program participants' personality and values through any

standard personality typing assessment tool (list under Resources section)

Potential Pitfalls

More seasoned employees may often feel that they do not have the time, energy or organizational support (including financial incentives) to train and support the junior participants in such a mentoring based program. To overcome this barrier, your company needs to make it possible for these senior-level staff members to participate using techniques like flexible scheduling or more work from home opportunities, in order to compensate for the time they spend participating in the program.

Guidelines for Coaching & Mentoring Success

- Create incentives – becoming a mentor can often be leveraged as a promotion. Offer hourly bonus increases to go through hands-on training, plus a larger bonus if the mentor completes a probationary period and another bonus if the mentor stays involved with the program a set period (usually a year, for ease in administering along with performance reviews) and conducts a certain number of mentor sessions.
- Make it a commitment – Provide mentor trainees with certain number of hours of training and participate in role playing and tests along the way.
- Encourage feedback – Seek out mentors as an invaluable resource on ideas to improve new employee orientation and training programs.

Post-Event Ceremony

Hold a graduation ceremony at the end of each session to acknowledge the participants.

Give plaques, certificates, and gifts to all program participants, such as books written by top performers focusing on workforce productivity, coaching or other relevant subjects.

Resources

- "A Mentoring Program to Reduce Turnover," Mark Noble, Best Practices in Aging Services.
- "Coaching, Counseling, & Mentoring: How to Choose & Use the Right Technique to Boost Employee Performance," Florence M. Stone.

Coach & Mentor Me Program Details:

Project Name:	**[Your Company Name] Coach & Mentor Me Program**
Project Owner:	Your Name
Start Date:	Month day, 2017
Complete By Date:	Month day, 2017
Business Units that Support the Program (If applicable):	
Business Sponsor (If applicable):	Typically Senior Management

Document Distribution:

Primary Contacts	Business Function
Name	Senior Management
Name	Finance
Name	Human Resources

Overview:

One of the greatest assets a firm brings to the marketplace is the collective intellectual capital of its employees. There is at present no way for [YOUR COMPANY] employees to submit ideas in a formalized process, for consideration, review, approval and action. We need to develop a process to systematically gather, assess, identify and sponsor (fund) exceptional ideas, via a cross-functional Team that is empowered by Senior Management.

By developing a formal process, we can harness the power of our people to gain long-term competitive advantage.

Goals and Objectives:

- Create a process to gather ideas from all areas of the organization.
- Develop a pre-funded program to back ideas for short and long-term marketplace competitive advantage.
- Develop cross-functional Team to review, process, streamline and facilitate the implementation of those ideas that will have an impact on the organization
- Develop intellectual capital.
- Long-term retain employees that might leave to pursue opportunities to leverage ideas for new products, services or businesses.

Metrics to Determine Success:

- Implement ideas to improve processes, improve efficiencies, streamline operations, reduce time to market, new products/ services, and other revenue generating or cost-reduction strategies to best leverage YOUR COMPANY for future success.
- Establish revenue objectives if applicable.

Themes /Messaging:

- Leverage Intellectual capital.
- Your voice is heard.
- You have to dream it to develop it.
- Our people are our inspiration.

Budget:

Item	Cost
Pre-fund the program for development, competitive information gathering, training, marketing, and other functions tied to launching and maintaining such a program.	$x,000

Reward contributors whose ideas have merit but cannot be pursued for various reasons.	$x,000
Reward contributors whose ideas are deemed worthy of implementation	$x,000
Total:	**$x,000**

Production Schedule:

Action	Start Date	End Date	Owner	Status
Senior Management needs to meet to discuss program parameters. Conduct during Strategic Planning process meeting. Identify likely participants for the cross-functional Project Team.	mm/dd/year	mm/dd/year	To be determined	Open
Share program details with the Company	mm/dd/year	mm/dd/year	To be determined	Open
First meeting of cross-functional Project Management Team.	mm/dd/year	mm/dd/year	To be determined	Open

Develop process for employees to submit ideas (email, fax, ftp server with an IDEA form?), and a system to generate automated replies. Then, you need a system to meet to review ideas, rate, rank and determine which to proceed with. Identify process for rewarding contributors (mention in newsletter, during Reward & Recognition program, etc.)	mm/dd/year	mm/dd/year	To be determined	Open
Develop idea submission form.	mm/dd/year	mm/dd/year	To be determined	Open

Promotional Campaign:

Initiative	Owner	Start Date	End Date	Status
Distribute internal email.	TBD	mm/dd/year	To be determined	Open
Promote program via Company newsletter.	TBD	mm/dd/year	To be determined	Open
Discuss during Town Hall meeting.	TBD	mm/dd/year	To be determined	Open

Contingencies Impacting Completion:

- Receive approval from Senior Management.
- Enlist participants of the Cross-Functional Team.
- Budget for pre-funding the program.

Develop a Training & Development Program

Your people are your business. They are the heart and soul of your company's brand, the front line facing clients, your image, the company's face behind your products and services...everything! Therefore, a top priority for your business should always be the development of your employees.

Before you develop an in-house training and development program, you will need to conduct an up-front skills assessment to identify specific metrics that will be employed, in order to define a successful program and to objectively assess employee increase in some pre-defined level of performance before and after the employee completes the program. Some metrics to apply when assessing the success of the training program on employee performance include:

- Increase in company standardized test scores
- Increases in productivity
- Feedback from program attendees' managers
- Improvements in performance as defined in specific skill categories

Some examples of how a Training Program can impact performance across the functional areas of your business include:

- Increase in data entry skills or a reduction in errors for administrative support staff.
- Increase in calls handled over a given time period, decrease in average per call time or increase in the number of calls successfully handled in a single session for customer care professionals.
- An increase in the number of records processed by medical billing professionals.

The selection requirements used to identify standards for employee participants need to be documented and communicated to your entire organization, to foster an inclusive program. You need to avoid the perception of, or the actual preferential treatment of, certain departments by including all employees. Two types of skill sets for development include hard and soft skills are ideal for development:

- **Soft skills**: Communications skills, team-building, problem-solving, presentation skills, project management skills, negotiating tactics, etc. These skills cannot be measured quantifiably.
- **Hard skills**: Task-oriented training to accomplishment specific technical requirements, measurable skill sets required from the job.

Training requirements vary by industry and by functional area so you will need to establish a program that adequately addresses the specific needs of a broad range of program participants. Some standards to apply include:

- Manufacturing firms require skills in kaizen-style lean manufacturing processes, which demand entirely new skill sets for production line workers to acquire.
- Companies in logistics management (ex. freight forwarders and shipping companies) need skills in all of the latest inventory management tracking and product flow management techniques.
- Finance professionals need to remain on top of the latest applicable regulations i.e. Sarbanes-Oxley compliance, ACH Check 21 rules and regulations, etc.

Prior to each session, the candidates enrolled in the campaign should have their performance review evaluated, with an emphasis on areas identified requiring improvement. The Train Me program committee assigned to implement the program should also revisit each participants' goals and objectives for the year, and the roles and responsibilities identified in the employees' job posting in order to determine potential areas for development.

A timeframe must be provided for the expected completion date of the program. Every employee enrolled in the program as well as their manager must sign an agreement, in order to confirm their participation in and commitment to the program.

Develop the necessary resources (written documentation, videos, assessment tools etc.) required to run the program.

Training & Development programs must be positioned as an incentive for those performers with long-term potential, and not as a punishment for sub-par performance. The program must be available to those folks dispersed in remote locations and cannot attend in-person.

Promote the Teacher Within

Companies derive the greatest collective benefit when their employees are the ones to conduct their training programs. It leads to greater employee morale, greater employee leadership skills development, better communications throughout the company, higher employer retention levels and lower costs since the training is conducted in-house. Employee-led training also leads to better content, since the people doing the training actually know the company (and its needs) best. Internal trainers have more credibility since they come from within the company and are better subject matter experts than outsiders. Content typically taught by insiders include: information technology, finance, leadership development, and performance management.

Employee teacher curricula should include why the material is important, what students need to learn during the program, and a plan for delivering it to the trainees. Employee trainers need to receive as much administrative support from the HR Department to implement the program as necessary, and trainers should work together, more senior trainer-employees mentoring junior-level trainer-employees. Employee trainers should be recognized and receive some benefits such as compensation or paid time off as incentives.

Training programs are especially effective to organizations when their employees are the ones to conduct the training.

In-Person vs. Distance-Based Learning

Today's wide range of e-learning technology options makes distance-based learning an extremely attractive option. For some employees, distance will be a challenge, and for others time is a primary constraint. Web-based training now helps companies of all types to overcome the challenge of information and knowledge sharing related to training.

HR professionals must be compelled to ensure that their employees receive specific training such as anti-sexual harassment and other types of mandatory training, which is simplified tremendously with the utilization of e-learning tools. The ideal scenario in which maximum results are achieved from training is when a combination of e-learning programs and traditional classroom style training courses are utilized.

Potential Pitfalls You Need to Avoid

Companies often compartmentalize a training program, by only engaging participants from one or several Departments which is typically Sales. They fail to gain a 360-degreee perspective by offering training to the entire organization's employees.

Resources

- Dr. Jack Phillips. Return on Investment in Training & Development Improvement Programs.
- Don Kirkpatrick. Measuring & Benchmarking Training.
- Tom Davenport. Thinking for a Living. How to get Better Performance and Results from Knowledge Workers by Harvard Business School Press.
- Leigh Branham. The Seven Hidden Reasons Employees Leave.
- Human Capital magazine – www.HumanCapitalmag.com
- Society for Human Resource Management – www.shrm.org (HR Magazine)
- Association for Talent Development – www.td.org

3. **Create a world-class culture** by leveraging WHY and WHAT IF as your organizational DNA. Encourage your employees to always ask "WHY" the organization does what it does, and also ask "WHAT IF" as a constant reminder that there are other ways of doing things, other potential solutions, and other innovative approaches to fuel your long-term growth. Identify the core values you want your organization to exhibit, then build a team of individuals that embrace those values.

4. **Hire the best talent** and find a place for them, instead of hiring to fill specific jobs. When you approach talent acquisition by only filling current vacancies, you are seeking employees with a finite skill set to deliver on the responsibilities of a specific "at that moment" job. Instead, teach all the Regions your organization sets up shop in how to hire the best talent and then make a place for them.

This way, you avoid falling victim to the sort of myopic, short-term approach of hiring in the moment that many organizations suffer from. Instead, take the long global recruiting approach of build the most powerful global teams with the collective skills, background, experience, training and interests that can be leveraged for competitive advantage but are not being recruited for.

5. For HR folks reading this, earn your seat at the management table by **delivering value on behalf of HR**. Human Resources has a rare and fading opportunity to deliver value to organizations they serve by seeing global organizational recruitment as an opportunity to infuse the organization with a new DIVERSE & GLOBALLY INCLUSIVE workforce. More about Human Resources later on.

6. Hire people who exhibit/possess a predefined set of **highly desirable employee attributes**, namely:

- Thrive in times of chaos;
- Are proactive;
- Can spot trends from seeming disparate events and connect seemingly unrelated data, events, data;
- Build and maintain strong relationships;
- Think unconventionally;
- Work well in teams AND independently; and
- Hire based on meaningful experience and NOT credentials (CV, grades,) or nepotism.

7. Implement **job rotations** as part of on-boarding and skills development to build stronger teams and maximize each employee's exposure to the entire organization.

8. Empower employees using **idea generation programs**. Workers closest to the customers and work processes and stakeholders should be able to make decisions independently for quicker responses to threats and to seize on opportunities.

9. **STOP preferential hiring**, promotions, and treatment (nepotism), once and for all. When you hire candidates based on pre-existing relationships or favoritism, you significantly REDUCE the talent pool by screening out potential TOP candidates.

10. **Hire, but…NEVER FIRE.** I LOVE being challenged by organizations and supposed leaders who cannot imagine a workplace in which you hire people for lifetime. Given that lifetime employment no longer exhibits, simply having this discussion opens up a dialog to what your values are, how valuable you see think your employees are, and how well you treat your people.

11. **Treat employees like customers and customers like employees**. Practice trust and transparency. Embrace ongoing organization-wide training and professional development programs that are tied directly to performance management plans that are meaningful to employees and map to your organization's short and long-term goals. Any/all programs must be measurable (think ROI) by directly and quantifiably impacting employee performance.

12. **Make ALL goals goldilocks or 'stretch' goals**. Goldilocks goals are "just right," meaning not too easy and not too challenging. They are ideal for most front-line staff and a majority of your people. For the rising stars, and most self-motivated, I urge clients to embrace STRETCH goals. A stretch goal is one that, even if you give that employee all the support, tools, resources, coaching, etc. to accomplish the goal, they still likely fall short. Why incorporate them, then? Because even if you "fall short" of achieving those lofty performance ambitions, they still will exceed your wildest expectations. The Rising stars in your organization (I refer to them as Superheroes) need/love to be challenged by seemingly insurmountable goals.

13. Institute job sharing, hoteling, and other employee empowerment best practices. Flexible work-life balance arrangements have nearly universal appeal to all FIVE segments of the American workforce but especially the Boomers and Gen Xers who are dealing with parents, children, grandchildren and loved ones that they need to care for.

14. Training should **embrace critical thinking and creative problem-solving**. Across cultures and country markets, having employees that can think independently, make sound decisions, and understand the stakes of their decision-making is invaluable.

15. Encourage risk-taking as part of your employee empowerment programs. Employees fearful of being punished for making wrong decisions will never take the calculated risks your organization needs, to maintain lasting competitive advantage. Seizing opportunities comes with inherent risk that can and should be effectively managed.

16. Build distance-based **virtual training programs** by leveraging technologies, tools, and resources. Technology enhancements continue to offer new professional development and skills enhancement to a globally dispersed workforce.

Here are some great resources to help you get started:

1. **Seven best collaboration tools** - http://worksnug.com/blog/7-best-collaboration-tools-for-virtual-teams.

2. **Ultimate list of virtual team technology tools** - www.thecouchmanager.com/the-ultimate-list-of-virtual-team-technology-tools.

3. **Working in a virtual team** - www.mindtools.com/pages/article/working-virtual-team.htm.

4. **Avoid cross-cultural faux-pas** - www.mindtools.com/pages/article/cross-cultural-mistakes.htm.

5. **The secret of successful remote working** - www.process.st/virtual-team-software.

6. **Top six (6) best practices for managing virtual teams** - www.corpedgroup.com/resources/pm/6BestPracticesMVT.asp.

What All This (Team Stuff) Means to Your Organization.

- The best (most productive) teams all share common characteristics.
- Successful teams are built on good leadership, trust, performance and rewards that reflect team-based contributions.
- Successful teams have members who believe in the team's mission and capabilities.
- It is often difficult to create team players when society rewards and promotes individual behavior.

5. Attitudes Matter

There are a number of factors to consider when determining the attitudes that employees feel about their work, the role they serve within their organization, how important their work is to themselves and others, and ultimately how engaged they are within their organization.

Job Satisfaction.

Are your people satisfied with the work they are doing? In my business consulting work, I often ask business owners to gauge the degree of satisfaction their employees have in the work they do. They often will ask why their people have to be satisfied, when they are being paid. Well, let's just say people who are satisfied work harder, take less sick leave, will work extra hours (unpaid), stay with your organization longer.

Job Involvement.

How "engaged" are they in their work? How much control/say do they have in their work. More on this later under the discussion of employee work autonomy.

Organizational Commitment.

The degree to which your people are committed to the ethics and values, of your organization. Do they attempt to promote your organization in the most favorable light, as Brand Ambassadors?

Perceived Organizational Support.

Do your people feel that your organization "has their back?" For example, what happens when your people feel they are being treated unfairly, and voice their concerns? Do they even feel comfortable expressing their feelings about poor treatment?

Employee Engagement.

It is instructive to note that determining how "engaged" your people are, requires your organization to have an understanding of EACH worker's motivation. Further, engagement is almost NEVER about compensation.

Employee Reward & Recognition Program.

Do you have a formal program funded with its own budget to reward and recognize your people? Is it tied to achieving your organization's highest goals, promote your values, and create a much more engaged workforce?

The single most important factor influencing an employees' level of satisfaction with their employer is the feeling of appreciation they receive. Employee retention and performance are directly linked to consistent, positive reinforcement via some reward and recognition mechanism.

When employees feel genuinely appreciated, they are more willing to stick with the company especially during hard times of economic hardship, when the company cannot afford to pay competitive salaries or offer aggressive bonuses or compensation.

Program Goals:

Establish criteria to define what goals you are looking to accomplish. Some goals might include:

- Increase employee retention – reduce your staff's annual turnover rate by a set % across the company or within specific functional areas.
- Generate employee goodwill – as evaluated using employee survey feedback data.
- Positive industry press coverage – determine how many press pick-up's your company will need to generate.

Conduct a Program Needs Assessment:

One easy step you can take to gauge overall employee satisfaction with the level of recognition your company provides is to ask them the following:

"To what extent do you agree or disagree with the following statement, 'My direct supervisor or manager does a good job recognizing my accomplishments.'

o   Strongly Agree
o   Somewhat Agree
o   Neither Agree nor Disagree
o   Somewhat Disagree
o   Strongly Disagree

Review all employee surveys that your people have completed, or create a survey specifically designed to determine if and how your employees have received recognition in the past. Find out if the experience was meaningful to them, and why it was/wasn't. If the recognition was not meaningful, then you will need to find out how to make it relevant, or the program will fail.

Organizational Benefits:

The benefits derived from establishing a reward and recognition program accrue not only to the participating employees, but also serve as an excellent tool for organizations to help them to: increase productivity, strengthen employees' focus on business goals, and defend the company against the employee attrition due to their dissatisfaction.

The cost estimates for employee turnover range from 53% - 150% of a lost employee's annual base salary. For a mid-sized company of 1,000 employees (with an average base salary of $55,000), assuming a 10% annual turnover rate, the total cost to the company would be $1.7 million to $7.5 million (SHRM).

The take-away? It is much more cost effective to do everything in your organization's power to ensure that your (best) people stay with you.

Company-Wide Adoption:

Building a recognition-based culture within your company means you have to make recognition a pervasive way of organizational life. In order to obtain company-wide acceptance, the program works best when recognition is applied in every direction. While the typical company recognition program is conducted in a top-down orientation with managers recognizing subordinates, direct reports must also be able to nominate managers, and recognition should also be encouraged on a peer-to-peer basis. Note that recognition is not a once a year event. It needs to be implemented on a regular consistent basis either monthly or quarterly to have meaning and change your organizational culture to a more "recognition" based model.

Establish an annual budget that receives approval from Senior Management for their "buy in". Hold a company-wide program. All offices must be invited, and there must be participation across the company from all Departments, either in-person (preferable) or else via videoconference to remote locations such as field offices. Tie all rewards given to performance-based metrics that reinforce the goals of the organization. Make sure that you do not exclude anyone, including contract/temporary employees. Selectively inviting only certain offices or departments creates ill will and resentment that will sabotage the program's goals and serve to reduce employee morale.

Award Ideas:

Give awards for individual and team-based performance. Here are some examples:

- Best process improvement.
- Highest sales / Highest sales increase over prior year.
- Most productive team project results achieved.
- Most outstanding service delivered.
- Best idea proposed to reduce organizational costs.

[NOTE: Ensure that sales awards alone are not given. Sales are often compensated on a commission basis, so awarding sales people might alienate other departments.]

Define the goals and objectives or the program. Publish and distribute the program's goals throughout the company by placing on the company intranet, as well as external website, include a mention in the company newsletter, include announcements with pay stubs, etc.

Guiding Principles:

- Rewards should be given for achieving significant outstanding performance.
- Most effective when the gifts are meaningful to the individual.
- Communicate and distribute rewards so they are not viewed as entitlements.

- Not a substitute for competitive salary structure.
- Rewards are not adjustments to base salary, supplemental compensation or variable pay programs.

Monetary vs. Non-Monetary Rewards

- The top 5 non-monetary reward-motivating techniques are:
- Congratulate employees when they do a good job.
- Writing personal notes about good performance.
- Using performance as a basis for promotion.
- Publicly recognizing employee for good performance.
- Holding moral building meetings to celebrate successes.

Potential Pitfalls:

Reward and recognition programs are not without potential drawbacks. Some potential pitfalls include:

- Measuring desired outcomes
- Matching the reward and recognition to the recipient
- Establish a return on investment to justify the program's impact
- Assess work/life centric forms of reward and recognition with such offers as:
  - Convenience services (onsite dry cleaning, daycare)
  - Paid time off
  - Wellness / fitness programs

Resources

- National Association for Employee Recognition.[46]
- Adrian Gostick & Chester Elton. A Carrot a Day.
- Jim Clemmer. How to Make Effort Rewarding.[47]
- World at Work 1999 Survey & Performance-Based Work Life Programs.[48]

---

[46] www.recognition.org

[47] www.clemmernet/exerpts/effort_rearding.shtml

[48] www.acaonline.org/research/generic/html/worklife_survey_name.html

Decision-making Involvement.

How much contribution do your people make into the decisions that affect their own work, the work of their team/Department, and your organization.

Idea Solicitation.

How aggressively do you solicit your people's ideas? They are the ones who are closest to your work flow, customers, vendors, suppliers. They should know best how to make the changes needed for your organization to not only survive but thrive.

The Big Idea. Daniel Pink. TED Talk: "Driving Employee Engagement." [49]

Employee Job Satisfaction Matters.

What is job satisfaction? It's that positive feeling you have about your work resulting from an evaluation of its characteristics. These factors entail the relationship you have with your Leader and/or peers, benefits, the autonomy you have over your job, pride in how your job and the organization you work for contributes to the societal greater good, health coverage, how challenging the work is, opportunities for advancement, rewards and recognition, the coaching and mentoring receive, your organization's investment in your professional training and development.

Clearly, when taken as a whole job satisfaction is much MORE than the tasks you complete day in and day out. For the average U.S. worker, job satisfaction remained consistently high from 1972 until 2006. Then what happened? The U.S. recession of 2007 – 2009, coupled with the mortgage foreclosure crisis. So much societal organizational employer goodwill vanished, because organizations lacked the compassion needed to put their people first.

When taking into consideration job satisfaction in multi-national corporations, it is important to know that measures of job satisfaction differ globally by culture, region, and job facet.

Work-Life Balance Across Cultures – A Study

---

[49] www.youtube.com/watch?v=x8PsRWvJz00.

In their study: "Outcomes of work–life balance on job satisfaction, life satisfaction and mental health: A study across seven cultures", researchers Haar, Russo, Sune, an Ollier-Malaterre investigated the effects of work–life balance (WLB) on several individual outcomes across cultures. Using a sample of 1,416 employees from seven distinct populations – Malaysian, Chinese, New Zealand Maori, New Zealand European, Spanish, French, and Italian – their research showed that WLB was positively related to job and life satisfaction and negatively related to anxiety and depression across the seven cultures.

Individualism/collectivism and gender egalitarianism moderated these relationships. High levels of WLB were more positively associated with job and life satisfaction for individuals in individualistic cultures, compared with individuals in collectivistic cultures. High levels of WLB were more positively associated with job and life satisfaction and more negatively associated with anxiety for individuals in gender egalitarian cultures. They concluded: "Overall, we find strong support for WLB being beneficial for employees from various cultures and for culture as a moderator of these relationships." [50]

Employee Engagement... a Definition:

Employee engagement is the extent to which employees feel passionate about their jobs, are committed to the organization, and put discretionary effort into their work. There are two primary factors which lead to employee engagement: 1) engagement with the organization; and 2) engagement with the employee's manager:

Engagement with The Organization measures how engaged employees are with the organization as a whole, and by extension, how they feel about senior management. This factor has to do with confidence in organizational leadership as well as trust, fairness, values, and respect - i.e. how people like to be treated by others, both at work and outside of work.[51]

Engagement with "My Manager" is a more specific measure of how employees relate to their direct supervisors. Topics include feeling valued, being treated fairly, receiving feedback and direction, and generally, having a

---

[50] www.sciencedirect.com/science/article/pii/S0001879114001110

[51] "What is employee engagement." www.custominsight.com/employee-engagement-survey/what-is-employee-engagement.asp.

strong working relationship between employee and manager based on mutual respect.

Compassionate Leaders Create Engaged Employees

People don't quit their jobs, they quit their bosses.2 It turns out that the opposite is true too. An inspiring manager creates more engaged teams. According to research by leadership development experts Dr. Brad Shuck and Maryanne Honeycutt-Elliott, **"higher levels of engagement come from employees who work for a compassionate leader—one who is authentic, present, has a sense of dignity, holds others accountable, leads with integrity and shows empathy".**[52]

> **It's not just about making them (employees) happy-that's not a business issue. Engagement is."** - *Julie Gebauer, Towers Watson*

According to the Harvard Business Review report conducted by interviewing 550 executives: **"The Impact of Employee Engagement on Performance,"** many organizations and their senior executives understand the need for achieving higher employee engagement. They just aren't sure how to measure it. The research found that while most leaders understand the importance of engagement, three-quarters of those surveyed said that most employees in their organizations are not highly engaged.

Not surprisingly, a significant gap showed up in the views of executive managers and middle managers in this area. Top executives seemed much more optimistic about the levels of employee engagement in their company, making them seem out of touch with middle management's sense of their frontline workers' engagement. Again, the higher up the organizational pyramid you go, the less in touch folks seem to be with what is actually going on with front-line, client-facing staff.[53]

The survey found that many companies find it challenging to measure engagement and tie its impact to financial results: fewer than 50 percent of companies said that they are effectively measuring employee engagement

---

[52] "7 Fascinating Employee Engagement Trends for 2016." David Mizne. www.15five.com/blog/7-employee-engagement-trends-2016.

[53] https://hbr.org/resources/pdfs/comm/achievers/hbr_achievers_report_sep13.pdf

against business performance metrics such as customer satisfaction or increased market share.

- 71% of respondents rank employee engagement as very important to achieving overall organizational success.
- 72% of respondents rank recognition given for high performers as having a significant impact on employee engagement.
- 24% of respondents say employees in their organization are highly engaged.

But one group of companies—called "high prioritizers" in the study because they saw engagement as an extremely important priority—are effectively using metrics and shared some best practices for tying engagement to business performance. These include:

- Avoiding rote surveys. Leading companies devote significant resources to carefully crafting employee engagement surveys so they ask pointed, clear questions that go beyond measuring "satisfaction." They then pore through the data to find the hidden stories of what's working and where there are pockets of dissatisfaction. Finally, senior management uses this information to inform strategy and policies going forward.
- Ensuring that goal alignment is occurring at every level of the organization and is well-communicated. Top managers set and communicate business objectives; middle managers are responsible for creating specific objectives for employees that support broader business goals; and employees are given the tools to succeed, some autonomy, and accountability to meet tangible goals aligned with corporate goals.
- Using data to leverage engagement initiatives to improve performance, typically customer satisfaction/net promoter score (NPS) surveys and feedback, and then tying winning results to recognition programs to reinforce alignment and the activities linked to performance. In most companies, today's leaders are acutely aware that there is much to be done to ensure that they have a focused and highly engaged workforce. Connecting engagement to business performance requires considerable effort

and top management focus—and, to a large degree, it is about how you do it. But there is enormous opportunity for companies that get it right.

Making Workers MORE Engaged.

There are some immediate steps that your organization can take if you wish to become a compassionate employer and reap the benefits of a fully engaged and committed workforce. Begin by creating an AMAZING culture, and strive to ensure that your people are doing meaningful work.

Reward and recognize them for outstanding achievement, exceeding goals, and representing your organization by exhibiting exemplary performance, values, and behavior. Solicit their ideas constantly, allow them to architect and manage their own work, create 360-degree performance reviews, and provide them with all of the tools, resources, support, and guidance that they need in order to succeed.

> **Train people well enough so they can leave, treat them well enough so they don't want to." -** *Richard Branson*

Make Your Workers Happy.

Worker happiness is an extremely nebulous concept to embrace, because happiness is an entirely personal perspective. Even two employees with very similar backgrounds performing the same job in the same Department perceive happiness in entirely different ways.

Fortunately, decades of research have revealed certain successful strategies for tapping into employee "happiness" as a means of unleashing their untapped potential and achieving maximum productivity for the organization's lasting competitive advantage.

Some organizations are becoming so focused on delivering employee happiness that they are creating a special new Senior-level title dedicated to employee happiness. Call it the Chief Happiness Officer.

What does such a grandiose titled individual actually do? A Chief Happiness Officer (CHO) is, in its essence, an HR Manager with a special qualification:

he/she believes happy employees make better employees. Engaging employees, motivating them and raising performance levels are all HR attributions. While these are the most common responsibilities used to describe the CHO position, there are many more HR areas where happiness matters.[54]

Every single action towards a person regarding their relation with the company, meaning all HR processes, can be re-defined to ensure a happy experience and a happiness-driven workplace. Recruitment and onboarding, career planning, performance management, succession management, engagement and recognition, off-boarding and retirement, these are all areas that can benefit immensely from a happiness-oriented approach.

Sound hokey? I get it. Sounds like a cross between Chief Cheerleader and Kindergarten teacher, combined with clowns, play dates, and birthday planner all rolled up into one. Well, quite a few organizations are dedicating the "C" suite Happiness title along with a focus on achieving organization-wide employee happiness.

Let's start at Silicon Valley. According to Laszlo Bock, SVP of People Operations at Google: "If you give people freedom, they will amaze you." But it's spreading. The Southern restaurant company Hopjacks created the CHO position in 2012.

Workplace Flexibility: allow your employees to set their own schedules for when (or even if) they commute to work, what hours they work, their daily/weekly schedules, who they decide to engage with in work teams, etc. Such flexibility is at odds with the tradition notion of work in that is grants significant autonomy to the individual to architect their work in such a manner as to maximize their own needs, wants, desires, strengths, and career goals.

> **"Research shows that people's happiness is affected by their sense of control over their lives. Being able to do your own work in your own way, or to influence your environment, gives a big boost in satisfaction."**
> -*Gretchen Ruben, Author, "The Happiness Project."*

---

[54] "What Does a Chief Happiness Officer Do?" Hppy. Paula Clapon. www.gethppy. com/hrtrends/what-does-a-chief-happiness-officer-actually-do.

Results-Only Workplace Environment (ROWE)

ROWE is a flexible workplace program first developed by Cali Ressler and Jody Thompson for Best Buy, but was terminated by Best Buy's CEO Hubert Joly in March, 2013.

ROWE was a ground-baking work program initiated by Best Buy to permit its Corporate non-store employees to work where and when they wanted, as long as they got their work done. According to Ressler and Thompson (who wrote a book and launched a firm, CultureRX, to spread their program), ROWE yielded impressive results.

Ressler and Thompson's research found that ROWE increases productivity, employee well-being, and work-life balance while decreasing turnover. At Best Buy, these results produced $2.2 million in savings over three years, according to the CultureRX website. The program has been implemented in 40 other organizations.

Why such notoriety among management thinkers and educators? Because ROWE systematically implements what decades of research studies have shown to be the keys to motivating and engaging a workforce for maximum performance, commitment, and satisfaction. It helps understand employee challenges and the work that needs to be done, gives them the autonomy, trust and support to accomplish objectives in the ways that work best for them, and provides feedback and recognition to let them know how well they're doing and reinforce good performance.

When implemented effectively by well-trained leaders, this is a recipe not only for promoting work-life balance, but also for maximizing the value and contribution of a firm's human capital over the long term.

Why then would Joly, Best Buy's CEO cancel the program? What killed ROWE at Best Buy was the same phenomenon that occurs frequently when a cost-cutting leader is appointed to turn around a struggling company. There is a short-term "get tough" mindset that gets employed, one that favors a rapid short-term improvement in the bottom line over the slower, more difficult — but ultimately much more powerful — work of developing and communicating a strategy and harnessing the talent and creativity of committed, engaged employees to implement it.

While cost-cutting efforts can boost a struggling company's stock price in the short term, it lays waste to human capital value — the very resource that is most critical in firms like Best Buy, whose fortunes depend on providing excellent customer service.[55]

Job Crafting

Confucius advised: "Choose a job you love and you will never work a day in your life." Steve Jobs agreed counselling: "The only way to do great work is to love what you do." The truth is a meta-analysis of almost one hundred different studies of working adults in almost every conceivable profession found that when our interests match our jobs we are generally more satisfied and happier with our lives.[56]

Job crafting allows employees to adjust their job to apply their skills, passions, and strengths. It is an effective way to unleash potentially untapped employee strengths and interests. You need two things to conduct effective job crafting: A compassionate organizational culture that strives to empower its people, and top talent that are self-motivated and driven to constantly explore creative new ways to architect their ideal work situation. For an in-depth explanation of how to unleash your people's untapped talents, see the Human Capital Audit section.

Creative ideas come from "putting new things in old combinations and old things in new combinations," according to organizational theorist Karl Weick. The concept of job crafting comes from that exact definition: If you take parts of your work and reconfigure it, you'll end up with a more meaningful job to better suit your talent and interests.[57]

Jessica Amortegui, Senior Director of Learning and Development at Logitech sees the following three essential requirements as being mandatory in order to conduct effective employee job crafting programs:

- Mastery – Making progress is what <u>researchers have found</u> motivates and engages people. This motivation is deeply

---

[55] https://hbr.org/2013/03/goodbye-to-flexible-work-at-be.

[56] "Can you teach someone to love their job." Michelle McQuaid.

[57] Vivian Giang. "Why innovative companies like Google are letting employees craft their own jobs." Fast Company. April 29, 2016.

rooted in a fundamental <u>psychological need</u> we all have to feel competent. Job crafting brings intention to this core motivational need by helping you look at the mix of tasks you're undertaking and where you're choosing to spend your time and energy.

Known as *task crafting* this can help you to identify what you're good at and how you can start honing these parts of your work. It also helps you to clarify the things you're not good at and that don't excite you and how you can find ways to minimize the time, effort, and energy you're putting into these parts of your job.

- Meaning – While most of us think that meaningful work starts with the work, <u>studies suggest</u> it actually starts with who our work impacts. It turns out that when you know your work has a positive impact on others, not only do you find a whole lot more meaning in what you do, but you're also far more motivated. Job crafting encourages you to step back from your daily to-do list and see the larger canvas on which your strengths, values and passions can be placed when it comes to having a positive impact on others.

  Known as *relational crafting* this can help you identify the interactions and connections that make your work meaningful, as well as those that make your work more challenging. It helps you to choose ways to invest in the relationships where you can make a positive difference, and to troubleshoot or limit contact in those undermine your sense of purpose.

- Membership – Felling socially connected is one of your most basic survival needs. As a result, <u>researchers are finding</u> that the more social you are the happier and more satisfied you feel. You make sense of your world through your relationships with others. Job crafting helps you to explore how your laundry list of job responsibilities fits into the larger goals of your organization so you feel that you're contributing to something larger.

Adam Grant has consulted with Google's *People Analytics Team* to help Googlers "customize" their jobs to make them more meaningful. Logitech and VMWare are two other organizations that use job crafting as a strategy to unleash its people's untapped potential.

Dissatisfied Workers.

There is a model that fits well with gaining an understanding of dissatisfied workers. It is called the **"Exit-Voice-Loyalty-Neglect"** Framework Model. Here is how it works:

- **Exit**: Unhappy people look to leave. Employees who are extremely unhappy are looking to leave and you likely do not know they are actively seeking external job moves.
- **Voice**: Attempt to improve conditions. Employees are still engaged but dissatisfied and will look to make the desired changes they think is best for themselves and the organization. How the organization responds determines if they decide to stay or leave.
- **Loyalty**: Optimistically waiting for things to improve. Your employees are still loyal to you, want to stay and will give your organization opportunities to fix what they perceive as being broken.
- **Neglect**: When employees feel that their work doesn't matter, they feel they are not being treated well, their ideas are not being solicited, and/or they are being micro-managed, they detach emotionally from the organization.

    In short, they stop caring. This is evident by a noticeable decrease in performance, and other signs of disengaging such as increased tardiness, sicknesses, or inter-personal issues arising with co-workers/peers, managers, and other stakeholders.
- The Satisfaction-Performance relationship is key, esp. in ***Customer Care*** roles.

There are significant and direct ties between employee job satisfaction and levels of customer satisfaction. Organizations that choose not to strive towards achieving employee happiness are choosing to jeopardize their relationships with and future profit derived from their customers.

Research examining the relationship between job satisfaction and job performance has been conducted since at least as early as 1945 (e. g., Brody, 1945) The idea that job satisfaction leads to better performance is supported by Vroom's (1964) work which is based on the notion that achieving employee performance is a natural outcome of satisfying the needs of your employees. The study relating to the relationship between job satisfaction and job performance has now become a research tradition in industrial-organizational psychology. The relationship between job satisfaction and job performance has been described as the "Holy Grail" of industrial psychologists (Landy, 1989).[58]

Job Satisfaction and Customer Satisfaction.

When an organization has happy employees, they have happy customers. That is truly one of the most important foundational cornerstones of the need for more compassionate organizations that treat their employees with respect and civility. It leads to stronger financial performance through a more highly engaged customer. Satisfied employees increase customer satisfaction and loyalty.

Take Zappos. The company's Number One core value is: "**Deliver WOW Through Service.**"

PROVIDE DETAILS OF ZAPPOS ICNREASE IN EMPLOYEE PERFORMANCE

Disney's mantra is "Create Happiness." It is built on a very powerful motto: "Treat employees like customers." [59]

Simply stated, your employees are your best **Brand Ambassadors**. Satisfied employees will be your most effective recruiters and PR function.

---

[58] www.questia.com/library/journal/1G1-325698274/relationship-between-job-satisfaction-job-performance.

[59] "One more time. How do you motivate employees?" Harvard Business School. Frederick Herzberg. January, 2003. https://hbr.org/2003/01/one-more-time-how-do-you-motivate-employees.

6. The Future Role of HR

What is and should be the role of Human Resources in today's compassionate organization? After all, many of the traditional roles served by HR including payroll and benefits administration, recruiting, employee training and development have been outsourced to various vendors including: Preferred Employer Organizations, recruiters and staffing agencies, training firms, consultants, etc.

When did HR abrogate its primary role of employee defender? Did it begin in the 1980s when they allowed manufacturing companies most notably the Big 3 American automakers to send hundreds of thousands of jobs overseas or down size millions of jobs in American Corporations in front-line staff and middle management?

Tasks that HR historically oversaw back when they actually worked to "earn" the HUMAN in their job titles included:

- Job Satisfaction and Absenteeism.
- Job Satisfaction and Turnover.
- Job Satisfaction and Workplace Deviance.
- Managers That Don't "GET IT".
- Employee Advocates vs Administrators?
- Preferred Employer Organizations Taking Over.
- Do They Affect Organizational Behavior and Culture?

HR can still be a powerful champion for employee happiness, motivation and empowerment. At the Chicago-based staffing and recruiting firm LaSalle Network, they view human resources as a partner to the business and their employees. The idea driving their pro-employee culture is that happy employees leads to happy clients.

A sub-team within their HR Department, the Human Concierge Department, exists to assist its new employees. Its HR employees provide the company's new hires with assistance in various life challenges such as: finding quality daycare and parental care, finding housing, and even getting a divorce.[60]

HR is especially needed when it comes to serving the needs of Millennial workers. Millennials are under different stressors than their older worker counterparts. They are the first generation to make less money than their parents, are beginning their careers with significant debt, and the first generation to grow up with social media. They may not mind posting about their lives but they are remiss to discuss it. Those born between 1979 and 1999 are struggling with depression in greater numbers more so than other generations, according to the American Psychology Association.[61]

Using Computers to Assess Human Emotions?

Affective Computing & Intelligent Computers

Technology has progressed to the point where computers can "read" the emotions your people are feeling. They can gauge your employee's emotions based on facial recognition, human-computer interactions. Such "Affective computing" can be leveraged by managers to keep their finger on the pulse of how satisfied your people are. Although there are of course ethical issues/considerations to overcome, a basic question that begs asking with respect to this growing technology is: "Why would/should ANY organization have to defer computers one of the most BASIC elemental requirements of our human condition?

---

[60] Workforce. May, 2017. Page 33.
[61] "Mental Health Takes on New Meaning for Millennials at Work." Rita Pyrillis. Workforce. May/June 2017.

7. Organizational Values

What Are Values?

A *value* per Milton Rokeach, U.S. researcher of values: "… an enduring belief that one mode of conduct or end-state of existence is preferable to an opposing mode of conduct or end-state of existence." "A *value system* is an enduring organization of beliefs concerning preferable modes of conduct or end states of existence along a continuum of relative importance."

Rokeach's work entailed organizing values into terminal and instrumental values. *Terminal* values are desirable end-states or goals for the organization to achieve. *Instrumental* values are the preferred or acceptable methods of behavior for employees to apply, in order for the employee, her Team, and the organization to achieve their terminal values.

Examples of *Terminal* and *Instrumental* values:

Milton Rokeach	
Terminal	**Instrument**
Property	Personal Discipline
Economic succes	Kindness
Enlightenment	Goal Orientation
Independent	Autonomy

The Organizational Imperative for Values

Compassionate organizations and their transformational leaders understand intrinsically the critical importance of building a strong foundation based on core values. To understand the impact of values on organizations, we need to first identify a few important terms:

- **Affect**: The broad range of feelings that people experience. An affect can be experienced as either emotions or moods.
- **Emotions**: Intense feelings directed at someone or something.

- **Moods**: Less intense than emotions, often arise without a specific event acting as a trigger.
- **The Structure of Mood**: Positive vs. Negative Affect.

Sincere Values Are Really Tough to Assess.

Business owners and CEOs claim that they care about core corporate values, and use buzzwords for values such as: "**Communication. Respect. Integrity. Excellence.**" These values sound great, right? Want to work for this organization? Before you answer, you might like to know that these are the stated corporate values of Enron, as listed in Enron's 2000 annual report. Remember Enron? As events proved, Enron's stated values weren't meaningful. Quite in fact, they were meaningless. The lesson is, quite often organizations are only paying lip service when they spew their values speak.

To find organizations who "walk the walk" with respect to values, it helps to ask: 'What do your values cost your organization?' For example, consider organizations that claim they value their employees. Ask if they have a no lay-off policy. Nucor Steel and Southwest Airlines avoided layoffs when they were struggling financially. They could have terminated employees, but they refused to do so because they place such a high value on their people.

When times get tough financially, does your Senior Leadership Team take a pay cut, or put off taking bonuses? How important is it for an organization to solicit and act upon the ideas its people come up with? If an organization is not willing to accept the pain that owning real values incur, they should not bother going to the trouble of formulating a values statement.[62]

Core values are the deeply ingrained principles that guide all of a company's actions. They serve as its cultural cornerstones. Jim Collins and Jerry Porras book "Built to Last" succinctly defined core values as being inherent and sacrosanct. They can never be compromised, either for convenience or short-term economic gain. Core values often reflect the values of the company's founders—Hewlett-Packard's celebrated "HP Way" is an example. They are the source of a company's distinctiveness and must be maintained at all

---

[62] https://hbr.org/2002/07/make-your-values-mean-something. Patrick Lencioni.

costs. [63] One of my all-time favorite organizations for core values is Patagonia. Their Mission Statement breathes its organizational values:

Our Reason for Being

"Patagonia grew out of a small company that made tools for climbers. Alpinism remains at the heart of a worldwide business that still makes clothes for climbing – as well as for skiing, snowboarding, surfing, fly fishing, paddling and trail running. These are all silent sports. None require a motor; none deliver the cheers of a crowd. In each sport, reward comes in the form of hard-won grace and moments of connection between us and nature."

"Our values reflect those of a business started by a band of climbers and surfers, and the minimalist style they promoted. The approach we take towards product design demonstrates a bias for simplicity and utility. For us at Patagonia, a love of wild and beautiful places demands participation in the fight to save them, and to help reverse the steep decline in the overall environmental health of our planet. We donate our time, services and at least 1% of our sales to hundreds of grassroots environmental groups all over the world who work to help reverse the tide."[64]

"We know that our business activity – from lighting stores to dyeing shirts – creates pollution as a by-product. So, we work steadily to reduce those harms. We use recycled polyester in many of our clothes and only organic, rather than pesticide-intensive, cotton. **Staying true to our core values during thirty-plus years in business has helped us create a company we're proud to run and work for.** And our focus on making the best products possible has brought us success in the marketplace."

Aspirational Versus Authentic Values.

Aspirational core values are those that an organization needs in order to succeed in the future, but currently lacks. An aspirational (new) value is often required, in order to support a new strategy, or to meet the requirements of a changing market or industry. Aspirational values need to be carefully managed to ensure that they do not dilute the organization's core values.

---

[63] Patrick Lencioni, HBR, July, 2002. "Make your values mean something."

[64] www.patagonia.com/company-info.html.

When Marissa Mayer was named CEO of Yahoo in July 2012, Yahoo's annual revenues had dropped from $7.2 billion to $4.9 billion in the previous four years. Employees were demoralized, and the culture was far from motivating. Mayer's answer to the company's poor performance was to proclaim that her goal was "to bring an iconic company back to greatness."[65] When an organization in financial in distress or undergoing transformational change sets aspirational goals it does so in order to clarify its goals and motivate its employees.

Authentic core values are the values that really, truly motivate your and your organization's current behavior. Sometimes these values lead to really wonderful, noble acts. Other times they lead to choices that we're ashamed of. They represent what is authentically true about the organization, both what is great and inspiring as well as what is purely fiction.

From the employee's perspective, the distinction between core and aspirational goals can be viewed in terms of the types of goal-setting the organization embraces. Organizations have been leveraging S.M.A.R.T. goals to improve employee performance and engagement and provide constructive feedback since they were first introduced into the workplace in the 1980s.

S.M.A.R.T goals stand for:

- **S**pecific: what do you want to achieve in your specific area of focus.
- **M**eaningful: Why is this goal important to you.
- **A**ction-Oriented: What steps will you take to achieve it.
- **R**ealistic: How do you know if you can achieve the goal.
- **T**imely: When do you want/need to accomplish the goal by.

However, there are a few reasons why SMART goals fall short in today's business climate:

- SMART goals emphasize the act of the goal setting, not goal pursuing.
- SMART goals stifle creative thinking.
- SMART goals limit **aspiration**.

---

[65] https://hbr.org/2017/01/the-stretch-goal-paradox.

While SMART goals are a major step up from not setting ANY goals and certainly still play a role in the goal setting process, leaders should consider moving to Objectives and Key Results (OKRs) as the primary goal setting model within their companies.

Perhaps the most important difference between OKRs and SMART goals is the link between OKRs and aspirational goal setting. The "A" in SMART which stands for "attainable," is often perceived as limiting and prohibitive to real growth. In fact, *a study conducted by Leadership IQ revealed only 15% of employees believe their current goals will help them achieve great things.*[66]

This lack of confidence in goals may likely be the result of the limiting nature of S.M.A.R.T. goals, which confine employees to what is considered to be realistic. OKRs, on the other hand, empower employees and businesses to set more ambitious goals and measure the progress they've made toward achieving those goals through measurable and time-bound key results.

Permission-to-play values simply reflect the minimum behavioral and social standards required of any employee. They tend not to vary much across companies, particularly those working in the same region or industry, which means that, by definition, they never really help distinguish a company from its competitors.

Values these days can be corporate social responsibility, supporting certain causes, being "eco-friendly" and offering employee benefits. These are all "me to" values, things most organizations do either because they have to or as a PR effort of good will to say: "Look how special we are" and "look how much we care." They are meaningless half gestures without much value.

Organizations, like individuals, possess values. Values drive an organization forward. After all, an organization is the collection of individuals who share ethics, beliefs, interests, and passions. As we head into the 21st Century, organization collective values are undergoing a transformational sea change especially in Compassionate Organizations.

---

[66] www.betterworks.com/articles/the-value-of-shifting-from-s-m-a-r-t-goals-to-okrs/

Organizational Changes in Values.

Past	NOW&FUTURE
Organizations USED to complete this way	NOW(AND IN THE FUTURE) they will complete on
Pricing	Employee engagement
Efficiency	Customer care
Cost-cutting	Values, ethics
Operations	Sustainability
FOCUS: Profile, Maximize SHAREHOLDER value	FOCUS: Profits for Purpose; maximize STAKEHLDERS value

The role of the organization has changed over the past few decades. In the past, organizations strived to achieve optimal operational performance in order to increase revenues, decrease costs, and achieve maximum levels of PRODUCTIVITY.

Under the old profit maximization model, primary focus was given to setting the right commercial pricing strategies, gaining organizational efficiencies, reducing costs (most often through Draconian lay-offs) running the organization's operations most effectively, and a singular focus on maximizing profits and ***shareholder value***.

PROFITS WITH PURPOSE.

Current and future trends outline a clear path forward for the **Compassionate Organization** to step in and drive our future economy forward. Key trends and developments include a need for employee engagement, a slavish devotion to an organization's customers, an emphasis on representing core employee values and operating with the highest ethical standards, sustaining the planet, and focusing on achieving ***PROFITS WITH PURPOSE***.

These changes embrace a VERY strong shift away from a singular emphasis on SHAREHOLDER value to maximizing all STAKEHOLDER value. Stakeholders are the groups of individuals that the compassionate organization "touches." Using this more expansive view that looks well beyond the customer, stakeholders range from employees and clients to the organization's partners (vendors, suppliers, contractors), the media, citizens, nature, non-profits, volunteer organizations, communities, and the planet.

Examples of Socially Progressive Organizations

Over the past decade, companies have started to realize that the pursuit of profit and purpose (aka social causes) can and should go hand in hand. Rather than separating the revenue-generating side of the business from the philanthropic side, socially progressive companies are thinking of them as co-existent, and in the process, generating greater impact and revenue than they would by keeping them separate. Four examples:

Uncharted Play

Jessica O. Matthews created the idea for an energy-harnessing soccer ball called the Socckrt while studying at Harvard. Realizing that the world of play was uncharted territory when it came to tangibly addressing real issues facing society, Matthews launched Uncharted Play in 2008. By 2015, Socckets are providing off-grid power to kids and families in rural and remote areas and refugee camps to improve learning, air quality, and health and increase income potential.[67]

Teeki

Founded by Lindsay Hemric in 2010, this eco conscious, activewear company makes its clothing from recycled plastic bottles. Teeki's style emanates not only from its good vibes–it's corporate ethos is summed up as: "we dance to a different beat, stretch with the yogi, run to the highest peak..."– but also from its commitment to support its customers with their active lifestyle to improve mind, body, and spirit. The company sources high quality materials that are conflict free, environmentally friendly and safe in order to improve the health and happiness of the earth and its people.

---

[67] "4 companies leading the next wave of profit with purpose." May 28, 2015. Phillip Haid.

Rareform

Founded in 2012 by brothers Alec and Aric Avedissian, the company manufactures surf bags, backpacks and totes from advertising billboards. By purchasing outdoor billboards before they discarded in landfills, Rareform creates unique, upcycled bags that reduce significant waste. Manufactured locally in California, the company was an immediate hit making a name for itself across 200 independent surf and sporting shops as well as national distributors like Patagonia and Whole Foods. As a member of 1% for the Planet, which means it donates 1% of its revenues, Rareform recognizes the interconnectedness between environmental degradation and the outdoor industry and is doing something creative to fix it.

LSTN

Founded in 2013 by Bridget Hilton and Joe Huff, this for-purpose company connects individuals, families and communities through sound. For every pair of headphones sold, they help restore hearing to a person in need through Starkey Hearing Foundation. LSTN believes that what's good for business should be good for the world so they set out to create a company that could create global change by providing high quality products that help fund hearing restoration and spread awareness for the global problem of hearing loss and hearing impairment. So far Hilton and Huff have given the gift of sound to over 20,000 people in the U.S., Peru, Kenya, and Uganda.

A 'Hall of Shame' of Lacking Corporate Values.

There are always examples of organizations that behave badly. Going back to the last American Recession of 2007-2009, we could easily identify Enron, Global Crossing, Adelphia. These days, there are plenty of organizations whose cultures are devoid of values and toxic environments of the most unethical behavior.

Uber's Track Record of Unethical Behavior.

When new employees join Uber, they are asked to subscribe to 14 core company values, including making bold bets, being "obsessed" with the customer, and "always be hustlin'." The ride-hailing service created by Travis Kalanick, Uber's former CEO particularly emphasizes "meritocracy," the idea that the best and brightest will rise to the top based on their efforts, even if it means stepping on toes to get there. Those values have helped propel Uber to one of Silicon Valley's biggest success stories. The company is valued at close to $70 billion by private investors and now operates in more than 70 countries.[68]

Yet the focus on pushing for the best result has also fueled what current and former Uber employees describe as a Hobbesian environment at the company, in which workers are sometimes pitted against one another and where a blind eye is turned to infractions from top performers.

This "blind eye" entails a culture of sexual harassment and discrimination, coupled with a history of aggressive anti-competition behaviors and ignoring local market rules and regulations. Senior level executives permitted top performers to treat female employees like playthings, and its drivers like replaceable commodities. Lawsuits filed by dozens of current and former employees include unwanted sexual advances and executives shouting homophobic slurs. Further, Uber said only recently in May, 2017 that it discovered an accounting error that it practiced that took extra millions of dollars in fees from its New York City drivers. In fact, evidence has recently come to light that Uber had known about its practice of deducting its commissions off driver pre-tax fares going back at least to 2015.[69] Ultimately, Travis Kalanick was forced out as CEO but as a major shareholder is working to fight his way back into the top seat at Uber.

Fair and Balanced Sexual Harassment at Fox News.

The pervasive culture of sexual harassment started at the top with Roger Ailes. Well done, Rupert Murdoch for permitting the fourth largest cable news network to not only condone but encourage Bill O'Reilly's sexual deviance in harassing numerous fellow female employees.

A *New York Times* investigation published in April, 2017 revealed that Fox News and Bill O'Reilly **paid $13 million** to five women since 2002 to settle harassment allegations brought against the Fox host. According to the report, the network and O'Reilly paid former female Fox contributors and employees to keep quiet about the allegations and drop any related legal suits. In addition

---

[68] www.nytimes.com/2017/02/22/technology/uber-workplace-culture.html?_r=0
[69] "Ube's Awareness of Error in Paying Drivers May Date to at Least 2015." Noam Scheiber. NY Times. June 2, 2017.

to the five settlements cited by the *Times*, two of which were already known, two other women spoke to the paper about O'Reilly's history of harassment, which included phoning women while apparently masturbating, trying to lure them to his hotel rooms, making lewd remarks, trying to kiss them, and hampering their careers when they rebuffed him. [70]

A Culture of Terror and Intimidation at Amazon.

Jeff Bezos is widely lauded for building an online book ecommerce site who took over borders online book ecommerce and parlayed that humble beginning into a global logistics and supply powerhouse. But the culture at Amazon can be seen for what it is. Amazon fosters a highly pressured performance driven environment that motivates employees through fear and the threat of employee termination that reduces employees to tears. Welcome to the world of Amazon as described by a New York times report in August, 2015:

Every Monday, new hires go through an orientation intended to launch them into Amazon's singular way of working. They are told to forget the "poor habits" they learned at previous jobs, one employee recalled. When they "hit the wall" from the unrelenting pace, there is only one solution: "Climb the wall," others reported. To be the best Amazonians they can be, they should be guided by the leadership principles, 14 rules inscribed on handy laminated cards. When quizzed days later, those with perfect scores earn a virtual award proclaiming, "I'm Peculiar" — the company's proud phrase for overturning workplace conventions.[71]

At Amazon, workers are encouraged to tear apart one another's ideas in meetings, toil long and late (emails arrive past midnight, followed by text messages asking why they were not answered), and held to standards that the company boasts are "unreasonably high." The internal phone directory instructs colleagues on how to send secret feedback to one another's bosses. Employees say it is frequently used to sabotage others. The tool offers sample texts, including this: "I felt concerned about his inflexibility and openly complaining about minor tasks." Not really compassionate, huh?

---

[70] www.slate.com/blogs/xx_factor/2017/04/03/the_fox_news_sexual_harassment_scandal_is_looking_worse_by_the_minute.html

[71] www.nytimes.com/2015/08/16/technology/inside-amazon-wrestling-big-ideas-in-a-bruising-workplace.html?_r=1

Many of the newcomers filing in on Mondays may not be there in a few years. The company's winners dream up innovations that they roll out to 250 million customers and earn small fortunes in soaring stock. Losers leave or are fired in annual layoffs - "purposeful Darwinism," one former Amazon human resources director said. Some workers who suffered from cancer, miscarriages and other personal crises said they had been evaluated unfairly or edged out rather than given time to recover.

It is hard to even attempt to explain such behavior other to say that Amazon's singular focus on achievement through innovation at all costs attracts a VERY specific type of employee. The informal culture Jeff Bezos has created is known and transparent, so employees who find such a culture attractive know what they can expect from a career perspective. One could make a convincing claim that it is difficult to argue with the company's tremendous success over the decades. But as noted repeatedly throughout this book, the mantra of sacrificing your people (culling the weak from the herd) for the financial performance of the company inevitably takes a negative toll on your people.

Killing Your Citizens, The Flint Michigan Way.

Nothing epitomizes the abuse of power more than knowingly poisoning your people's drinking water with toxic levels of mercury. And yet that is exactly what the City of Flint, Michigan did.

When Flint's water started smelling foul, tasting odd, turning orange and the children drinking it started to develop nasty skin rashes, there was clearly something terribly wrong. But what? That was a mystery that only chemistry could solve. In the spring of 2014, large amounts of lead found their way into the water that some residents of Flint, MI, were using to drink, cook, and brush their teeth. Lead is known to be particularly damaging to young children's developing brains. So how did lead get into the tap water in Flint?

Treating and supplying water

In **early 2013,** in order to save money, Flint officials decided to change the source of the city's water from the Detroit Water and Sewerage Department to the Karegnondi Water Authority (KWA). However, KWA was not ready to deliver the water, because they were in the process of building a new pipeline to bring water from nearby Lake Huron. This meant that officials in the city of Flint needed to find a short-term solution while the new pipeline was being built. They decided to use water from the local Flint River that they would clean in water treatment plants.

In **April 2014,** Flint switched over to the new source, and the problems began almost immediately. Within weeks, residents were complaining of foul-smelling and discolored water. The city initially denied that there were any issues, but within a few months, they issued a boil-water advisory. Later, in **October 2014,** the General Motors car plant in Flint announced that they would no longer use the water, because they feared it would cause corrosion within the factory.

A few months later, Flint told its residents that their water had high levels of organic molecules called trihalomethanes. These molecules are similar to methane molecules (CH_4), but three of the hydrogen atoms are replaced with halogen (group 17) atoms—fluorine, chlorine, bromine, or iodine. The four most common trihalomethanes are dibromochloromethane ($CHClBr_2$), dichlorobromomethane ($CHCl_2Br$), trichloromethane ($CHCl_3$)—better known as chloroform—and tribromomethane ($CHBr_3$).

Trihalomethanes are a concern because they have been linked with numerous health concerns, including liver, kidney, lung, and heart problems. When the chorine used to disinfect water reacts with algae, leaves, and weeds, trihalomethanes are produced.

Toxic levels of lead

Trihalomethanes are just one group of chemicals associated with water contamination, lead is another. Lead was a popular choice for use as water pipes for centuries. The Romans used the dense metal because of its durability and malleability. Water pipes are no longer made from lead, but older cities, such as Flint, still rely on lead pipes—in addition to those made from copper and iron—to transport water to people's homes. In Flint, massive levels of lead entered the water system. In one sample of water taken from a Flint home, a lead level of 13,000 parts per billion (ppb) was found. The chemists who tested the water were skeptical at first. But after repeating the experiment a number of times, they found that the 13,000 ppb reading was accurate.

It is important to note that no level of lead in the water supply is considered safe, but the U.S. Environmental Protection Agency has set a maximum level of lead contamination in the tap water in 90% of homes at 15 ppb—also known as the "action level." That particular sample of Flint water had a lead level close to 1,000 times the action level.

So, four entirely different organizations and circumstances yet one overlapping similarity exists in these and other organizations that practice such unethical behavior. An awareness, tacit approval or outright participation in such unethical behavior at the highest levels of the organization.

8. Ethical Behavior in Your Organization

Ethics...a definition:

"Being in accordance with the accepted principles of *right* & *wrong that govern the conduct of a profession.*" [72]

Ethics is "...the ability to monitor one's own and others' feelings and emotions, to discriminate among them and to use this information to guide one's thinking and actions." Peter Salovey & John D. Mayer [73]

Treat Your Employees Like Strategic Partners

Goodbye and fond farewell to the 20th Century command-control pyramid-shaped organization. Gone is the Corporation whose sole purpose for existence is the pursuit of profit at any and all costs. Welcome to the new *"compassionate organization"* that is required for lasting competitive success in the 21st Century.

And while it may take global banks, financial institutions, petroleum companies, gun manufacturers, tobacco companies, and other less than ethically based institutions some time to discover this phenomenon and adapt to the new reality of the compassionate organization, the landscape is ALREADY changing and quickly.

Global trends will further expedite the shift to a more ethical, cause-based socially conscious organization. Trends like global competition, social media, the sharing economy, a pervasive "war" for top talent, sustainability, rapid idea diffusion through the Web, virtual reality, augmented reality, artificial intelligence, and the near constant rate of technological innovation the old ways of focusing on maximizing profit and treating employees like assets akin

---

[72] www.thefreedictionary.com/ethical.

[73] http://psychology.about.com/od/personalitydevelopment/a/emotionalintell.htm

to photocopiers with limbs. The profit above all else mantra and Greed is Good mindset no longer serves as a viable lasting competitive business model.

Many of the foundational underpinnings of this kinder, more caring organization have been in place for some time. Compassionate organizations can be identified by the type of flexible work arrangements they offer to their employees. These caring organizations put employees first every day by allowing their people to work where and when they feel they are most productive, give them time off to solve their organization's (and society's) problems, come up with innovative new products and services, solve problems and architect their OWN work as they see fit.

These compassionate organizations are re-aligning their organizations by removing 20th Century pyramid-shaped command and control organizations. In its place, leaner, less hierarchical flatter MATRIX organizations with self-directed/self-managed work teams are forming in lieu of traditional management structures.

The new compassionate organization encourages its employees to pursue outside interests and achieve self-actualization through community engagement, volunteer work and giving back to their communities. Need examples? Following is merely a short list of compassionate organizations who comprise an enlightened employer '**Hall of Fame**':

+Patagonia	+Zappos
+Wegman's	+DuPont
+Edward Jones	+Johnson & Johnson
+Chobani	+WL Gore
+Kind	+UPS
+Whole Foods	

For a more comprehensive list of these compassionate organizations, I suggest that you refer to the **Fortune 100 best companies to work for.**[74]

The most compassionate organizations understand that they make a powerful commitment to their employees when they extend an offer of employment. It is a partnership that enlightened organizations make VERY seriously. One

---

[74] http://beta.fortune.com/best-companies.

way to begin framing your employee relationship differently is to consider *treating employees like your most loyal customers.*

Employees are most definitely **NOT** assets to be managed. The idea of an employee as an asset has significant negative connotation and indicates the organization or executive who makes such a statement is not in the least empathetic towards their people.

The concept of employee as organizational asset implies that they are in effect human photocopiers with limbs to be disposed of at will. They are pushed to maximize their own productivity, and then can be discarded ("depreciated") at the whim of their manager when they are deemed expendable.

As a completely contradictory ethical guide, I coach my clients to hire the BEST and NEVER downsize! Ethical organizations understand the similarities and the differences between the 5 generations of U.S. workforce: Matures, Baby Boomers, Generation Xers, Millennials/Gen Y, and the iGeneration/Generation Z.

Provide your people with financial advising, and offer/arrange flexible work schedules. Set up a retirement plan that allows applicants to match contributions **up to 4%** of their income. Empower your people to determine/manage their own learning, and provide them with tools they need to succeed. Don't TELL employees to act like OWNERS. EMPOWER them to BE ownership. The end game for the compassionate organization is to help its employees achieve a higher sense of purpose.

Most organizations deal with ethics and being ethical (if they deal with ethics at all) by lumping them together into an "Ethics and Compliance" program and having the program managed by a Compliance Officer, their in-house Corporate Counsel, and/or their law firm.

To determine if an organization has a high moral (ethical) compass, it helps to assess their corporate policies. For example, look at Salesforce. com. For years, **Salesforce.com** has been honored for its philanthropy and good practices. Through its Salesforce.com Foundation, the company has donated millions of dollars toward education grants and technology, and even discounts its services to non-profit organizations. The company also encourages its employees to get into the action by giving them six days off per year to do any type of charitable work they choose. Saleforce.com frequently ranks highly on lists of companies offering the best salaries and hourly rates for employees.[75]

SAS Institute is another software company that is renowned for its employee benefits. Employees at SAS receive subsidized Montessori child care, unlimited sick time, and access to a free health center. The company also fosters a strong sense of community; its staff has intramural sports leagues, and the company has never had a layoff. SAS also supports education philanthropy, particularly programs that are dedicated to promoting science, technology, engineering, and mathematics programs for children. The company encourages its employees to volunteer at various charities and even makes cash contributions to non-profit programs where the employees volunteer.[76]

CEO John Mackey of Whole Foods created a non-profit called Conscious Capitalism specifically to spearhead the altruistic ambitions of its organization.

And then there is Microsoft. Given the fact that it was started by Bill Gates, one of America's most generous philanthropists, it follows that Microsoft behaves in such an ethical manner. The tech company and its employees donate over $1 billion yearly to charities and non-profit organizations and the Bill and Melinda Gates Foundation are globally renown philanthropists. If that wasn't enough, Microsoft's management and employees have also decided to tackle America's shortage of IT professionals through its TEALS program.

Through the TEALS program, Microsoft employees are encouraged to volunteer at local schools to instruct students in computer science, in the hopes that it will inspire them to enter the technology industry. It's only natural that Microsoft employees would be generous people; in addition to being among the highest paid employees in America, they also enjoy a plethora of perks, including 100% coverage on their health care premiums.

Ethical Organizations are MORE Profitable.

Need proof that there is a growing global trend afoot for the 'for-profit' company to shift its focus from pure profit maximization to more ethical and

---

[75] www.minyanville.com/sectors/consumer/articles/Good-Business253A-Corporations-with-Great-Ethical/2/16/2013/id/48045.

[76] www.minyanville.com/sectors/consumer/articles/Good-Business253A-Corporations-with-Great-Ethical/2/16/2013/id/48045.

compassionate behavior? The **Ethisphere Institute** (www.ethisphere.com) has been researching the financial performance of ethical organizations for over a decade now. From the home page of their website:

"At Ethisphere, we know that doing the right thing is not always the road most easily traveled. That's why we honor those companies that do it. It takes grit to enact policies that are forward-thinking rather than focused on short-term gains. It takes fortitude to make the right decision even when the ethical call can hurt the bottom line and it takes foresight to understand the difference and appreciate the long-term value. As we compare the 2017 World's Most Ethical Companies honorees to the S&P 500 over the last 2 years, the gap (6.4% to the positive) is palpable – we call it the **Ethics Premium.***"*

They collect ethics survey data from thousands of organizations. Their research has uncovered an amazing phenomenon. Organizations globally that perform the most "ethically" consistently outperform financially their less ethical competitors across all industries and countries.

Think this is a fluke? Think again! Compassionate organizations are ideally positioned to pursue corporate purpose by unleashing their people's untapped potential for lasting competitive advantage.

LOOKING FOR A LACK OF ETHICS? SEE THE AUTO MAKERS!

For proof of a prevailing lack of ethics that exist in many corporations, we need look no further than automobile manufacturers. On May 18, 2017, Fiat Chrysler said it was in discussion with the U.S. Department of Justice to settle an investigation into diesel deception amongst mounting evidence that it used illegal software to evade emission tests.

Volkswagen had already gone through a similar diesel emissions testing manipulation scandal, and has already been hit with billions of dollars in settlements and fines. Software in both automobile manufacturer's engine computers were found to reduce pollution controls after vehicles were started, thus falsely appearing appear to comply with national emission standards. [77]

The automotive world was rocked by a massive airbag recall covering millions of vehicles in the U.S. from nearly two dozen auto brands. The issue involves

---

[77] "Fiat Chrysler Seeks a Deal as VW's Pain Looms Large." Jack Ewing. New York Times. May 19, 2017. Page B1.

defective inflator and propellent devices from Japanese supplier Takata, that may deploy improperly in the event of a crash, shooting metal fragments into vehicle occupants. What!?! Approximately 42 million vehicles are potentially affected in the United States, and at least 7 million have been recalled worldwide.[78]

Defective airbags made by Takata have been tied to at least 11 deaths and over 180 injuries in the United States alone. The ensuing recall — the largest in automotive history — has been confusing and frustrating for car owners.[79] A device intended to SAVE people's lives in the event of a crash actually serves as an IED (Improvised Explosive Device) to potentially kill or maim the riders in a vehicle involved in said crash? Hmm.

Initially, only six makes were involved when Takata announced the fault in April 2013, but a Toyota recall in June, 2016 - along with new admissions from Takata that it had little clue as to which cars used its defective inflators, or even what the root cause was—prompted more automakers to issue identical recalls. In July, the NHTSA forced additional regional recalls in high-humidity areas including Florida, Hawaii, and the U.S. Virgin Islands to gather removed parts and send them to Takata for review.

Another major recall expanded the affected vehicles to additional brands. For its part, Toyota said it would begin to replace defective passenger-side inflators. If parts are unavailable, however, it has advised its dealers to disable the airbags and affix "Do Not Sit Here" messages to the dashboard. Well… that's helpful.

It seems like the American auto manufacturers want to get into the act. A Seattle, WA based law firm that specializes in suing auto manufacturers has filed a class action lawsuit against General Motors, accusing the company of programming some of its heavy-duty trucks to cheat on diesel emission tests.[80]

The Banks and Financial Services Firms Never Learn.

---

[78] http://blog.caranddriver.com/massive-takata-airbag-recall-everything-you-need-to-know-including-full-list-of-affected-vehicles/

[79] www.nytimes.com/interactive/2016/business/takata-airbag-recall-guide.html

[80] "G.M. Cheated on emissions tests, lawsuit says." NY Times. May 27, 2017. Neal E. Boudette.

Deutsche Bank has been fined $630 million to date after illegally laundering $10 billion in dirty Russian bank money.

Walmart, Not Very KIND.

A report of more than 1,000 Walmart employee surveys released on Thursday, June 1, 2017 by a worker advocacy group reported that Walmart routinely refuses to accept doctors notes, penalizes workers who need to care for sick family members, and otherwise punishes its employees for lawful absences from work. The report accuses Walmart of violating the Americans With Disabilities Act and the Family and Medical Leave Act.[81]

Compare such treatment of employees by Walmart with the practices of KIND, as set for in the book "Do the KIND Thing" by author and company CEO Daniel Lubetzky. Inspired by his father, who survived the Holocaust thanks to the courageous kindness of strangers, Lubetzky began his career selling a sun-dried tomato spread made collaboratively by Arabs and Jews in the war-torn Middle East. Despite early setbacks, he never lost his faith in **his vision of a "not-only-for-profit" business—one that sold great products and helped to make the world a better place.**[82]

Lubetzky doesn't believe you should call your workers 'employees.' "We don't use the term employee at KIND because it has kind of acquired this connotation of subservience," he says. At KIND, we are all team members. Nobody works for me. They work *with* me, I work *with* them."[83]

KIND, which launched in 2004, has sold more than one billion bars and currently has 300 people working full-time at the company. Every full-time team member begins receiving stock options as soon as their new hire paperwork is processed. The equity in the company vests over time. "Ownership mentality is extraordinarily important at KIND," Lubetzky says. "It's probably one of the most important aspects of our culture and of the way we do things."

Even KIND's social media posts are…well…kind.

---

[81] "Walmart is Accused of Punishing Workers for taking sick days." The NY Times. June 3, 2017. Rachel Abrams. Page B-3.

[82] www.kindsnacks.com/do-the-kind-thing-book

[83] "Why the Founder of KIND Doesn't Use the Word Employee." Catherine Clifford. Dec. 20, 2015. www.entrepreneur.com/video/253697.

9. Motivation

What is Motivation?

Do you want to encourage and inspire motivation in your people? Maybe you'd like to better understand what motivates you? Either way, we first need to know what motivation is and isn't.

Motivation is an employee's intrinsic enthusiasm about, and their drive to accomplish, activities related to their work. Motivation is an internal drive that we all possess. It causes us to strive for excellence. Motivation drives us to take action, or in the absence of it leads us to be no more than passive witnesses to the world around us.

An individual's motivation is influenced by their personal identity, the collection of biological, intellectual, social and emotional factors that makes each of us truly unique. This means, we are all motivated by different factors. Therefore, motivation is complicated. It's not easily defined, and it's an intrinsic driving force that can be influenced by external factors and is different for every single individual. [84]

Every person is motivated differently. Every employee has activities, events, people, and goals in their life that they find motivating. So, motivation exists in each of us. Compassionate organizations "get" this and create a culture that strives to understand what motivates each employee they make a work contract with and use motivation to help their employees achieve at their highest potential.

In his TED talk "The Puzzle of Motivation," Career Analyst *Daniel H. Pink* discusses his findings from the science of human motivation, and the difference in intrinsic and extrinsic motivators with the power of incentives. Research into human motivation is conclusive that if you want to motivate people to engage and perform at a much higher level, then you need to tap into their intrinsic motivation. Further, he emphasizes that there is a tremendous

---

[84] "What is Employee Motivation?" Susan Heathfield. August 26,2016. www. TheBalance.com.

difference in what science already knows, and how MOST businesses are still foolishly locked into extrinsic approaches to employee motivation. [85]

Why Motivation Is So Important to Employees.

Employees who are motivated by the belief that their work has meaning and they feel challenged are more driven to excel at their work. Employees take greater pride in the quality of their work when they can understand how the work that they perform fits with the work of their Team, and their organization as a whole. The challenge all compassionate organizations embrace is to determine how to give an employee's work meaning.

Why Motivation Matters to Employers.

When employees are motivated they are in a place where they are challenged by work that demands their full attention, requires them to stretch themselves to their maximum capability, and are doing work that demands they apply all their prior training, skills and abilities. In his TED talk: "Flow, The Secret to Happiness" *Mihaly Csikszentmihalyi* refers to that state of work-related challenge/nirvana as being in a state of FLOW.

Csikszentmihayi explains his use of psychology as a means of researching people who find pleasure and lasting satisfaction in activities that bring about a state of "flow." He defines "flow" as a state of heightened focus and immersion in activities such as art, play, and work. [86]

When employees are most effectively motivated, they work at optimal levels of capability and efficiency and their organizations derive the greatest possible return on their people investment. Motivated employees take less sick time, are willing to work for less than maximum pay, stay with the organization longer, contribute (invest) more of themselves for the benefit of the organization, refer top performing friends to the organization, and positively promote their organization to their social and professional peers.

The seven indicators of people being in a state of "FLOW" *Csikszentmihalyi* identified are:

---

[85] www.ted.com/talks/dan_pink_on_motivation#t-307131.

[86] www.ted.com/talks/mihaly_csikszentmihalyi_on_flow.

1. Completely involved in what they are doing – focused, concentrated.
2. A sense of ecstasy – of being outside everyday reality.
3. Greater inner clarity – knowing what needs to be done, and how well we are doing.
4. Knowing that the activity is doable – that our skills are adequate to the task.
5. A sense of serenity – no worries about oneself, and a feeling of growing beyond the boundaries of the ego.
6. Timelessness – thoroughly focused on the present – hours seem to pass by in minutes.
7. Intrinsic motivation – whatever produces flow becomes its own reward.

Does this sound like your work? Given all the positive benefits that organizations achieve by motivating their people, why WOULDN'T they do everything in their power to motivate their people Following are the best practices that an organization should consider employing to produce a highly-motivated workforce.

Job Design

Job design entails empowering each person in your organization to design a set pattern of work that enables your people to achieve their full potential in such a manner that allows them to express their ethics, act in a moral manner, engage in their work as the OWNER of their work.

It encompasses their ability to architect their roles and responsibilities, engage others to work in teams as they see fit, and be the ultimate owner of their own individual performance for the greatest good of the organization. Job design is the ultimate 21st Century transformative work model. Job designing demands organizations that embrace it possess visionary leaders, a long-term commitment to employee success, and the ability to hire the Superheroes needed to thrive and succeed in such self-directed, self-managed work engagements. Truly powerful stuff, indeed.

The Job Characteristics Model

The job characteristics model was developed by J. Richard Hackeman and Greg Oldham. **Job characteristics theory** is a theory of work design. It provides "a set of implementing principles for enriching jobs in organizational settings". The original version of job characteristics theory proposed a model of the following five "core" job characteristics:

This model can be used to describe **ANY** job along **5** key dimensions:

- **Skill variety**: degree to which the job requires different activities requiring specialized skills and talents
- **Task identity**: Does the job require you complete an entire piece of work. In the assembly line model individuals performed merely one task out of many.
- **Task significance**: Degree to which the job affects the lives or the work of others.
- **Autonomy**: Does that job provide the worker with freedom, independence, and discretion in the scheduling and arranging of their own work.
- **Feedback**: The employee receives guidance and input on their job performance.

These core job characteristics affect work-related outcomes (motivation, satisfaction, performance, absenteeism and turnover) through three psychological states: 1) experienced meaningfulness; 2) experienced responsibility; and 3) knowledge of results.

Motivation Potential Score

MPS is a predictive index that suggests the motivating potential in any job for any worker in your organization. Motivation, it turns out can actually be calculated and measured by applying the following formula:

MPS = Skill Variety + Task Identity + Task Significance x Autonomy X Feedback / 3

To be high on motivating potential, a job MUST be high on AT LEAST one of the 3 factors. The MPS model does have merit, BUT you can better calculate a job's motivating potential by simply totaling the 5 factors for one aggregate score. Test out which approach works better for your organization by first applying the formula, and then by adding up the 5 factors to see which works better.

Regardless of the approach you take to calculate motivation, the take-away to note is that motivation once deemed impossible to quantify can in fact be measured. The true question is, does your organization care enough about its people enough to go through the significant effort to gauge overall employee motivation.

Redesigning Your People's Work

Redesigning your people's work to make their work more challenging, meaningful, and thus motivating can be accomplished using a number of strategies.

Steps to the Job Redesign Process:

- **Revise the Job Content:** Begin by gathering the employee's job-related information to uncover any inconsistencies between the employee and their job.
- **Analyze Job-related Information:** Once you have successfully completed the collecting and revising of the job's "content", analyze the discrepancies between what the employee is tasked with doing and what they are capable of doing. You go through this process in order to determine any potential barriers preventing the employee from successfully performing job-related tasks and duties and investigate why an employee is not able to achieve their desired goals.
- **Alter the Job Elements:** The next step is to adjust the job's roles and responsibilities. It may include removing extra responsibilities, adding more functions and a higher degree of accountability and/ or offering the employee training and professional development opportunities as well as support resources. The goal with altering the job's requirements is to design work in such a manner that encourages employees to work harder, perform better, remain motivated and engaged, and thus achieve higher employee retention, satisfaction, and performance.
- **Redesign the Job Description and Specifications:** After altering the job elements, you will need to change the job description and

specifications, in order to make sure that the worker placed in that role is able to deliver what is expected of them.

- **Re-order Job-related Tasks and Duties:** Next is to reallocate new or altered tasks and functions to the employees' performance management plan. It may be done by rotating, enriching, enlarging and engineering the job. The idea is to motivate your people while increasing their satisfaction.

The Benefits to Job Redesigns:

- **Enhances the Quality of Work-Life:** Job redesigning motivates your employees and enhances the quality of their work-life balance. It increases their on-the-job productivity and encourages them to perform at a higher level.

- **Increases Organization's and Employees' Productivity:** Altering employee job functions and duties makes employees much comfortable and adds to their satisfaction level. The unambiguous job responsibilities and tasks motivate them to work harder and give their best effort. This in turn results in overall organizational increased productivity.

- **Brings the Sense of Belongingness in Employees:** Redesigning jobs and allowing employees to do what they are best at creates a sense of belonging in them towards your organization. It is an effective strategy to retain your people and encourage them to carry out their responsibilities, while achieving your desired end goal of them contributing to their Team and organizational goals.

- **Creates a Right Person-Job Fit:** Job Redesigning plays an important role in creating a culture driven by "right person-job fit" while harnessing the full potential of EVERY one of your employees.[87]

[**NOTE:** For a detailed description on how to conduct a job redesign, check out the chapter "Human Capital Audit".]

---

[87] www.managementstudyguide.com/job-redesign.htm

Job Rotations and Cross-Training.

Periodically shifting an employee to different departments, job functions, or office locations is an extremely effective strategy for assisting employees in mastering new skills. Organizations that practice employee rotations achieve better performance from employees. Job rotations are especially beneficial for and applicable to assembly line workers and new managers.

Why offer rotations and cross-training your people? It reduces boredom, increases motivation, aids workers in understanding how their job fits with others on their team and in the organization, and reduces dependence on workers with sole knowledge of tasks, all leading to greater org. performance.

Job Enrichment Programs

Job enrichment programs allow employees to increase the degree to which they control the planning, execution, and evaluation of their own work.

Such programs enable workers to do entire range of all tasks associated with the job increases employee freedom and independence, increased responsibility and feedback to assess and correct their performance. Some successful methods to enrich employee jobs include: combining tasks, form natural work units, establish client relationships, expand the job vertically to higher levels with tasks typically held by managers, and constant, open feedback channels between team members, as well as up and down the organizational structure.

Relational Job Design

An extremely powerful tool for motivating employees is relational job design (RJD). With RJD the organization focuses on creative ways to make its people's jobs more "pro-socially" motivating to its employees. The goal here is to architect work in such a way that employees are motivated to promote the well-being of the organization's beneficiaries/stakeholders (such as clients, patients, employees, vendors, etc.)

In so doing, the organization achieves a powerful goal of effectively "connecting" its employees with the beneficiaries of their work. Employees derive tremendous benefit in that they get to see first-hand how their work affects people's lives.

Take for example Call Centers staffed with employees whose goal it is to conduct ongoing, repetitive tasks of soliciting donations as part of ongoing fundraising efforts. One effective strategy under RJD would be to have people who benefit directly from the fundraising efforts give motivational speeches to those employees how the donations they solicited changed their lives for the better.

Alternative Work Arrangements

Giving employees the option to work when they want, where they want, and in the manner in which they wish empowers employees with autonomy and thus direct control over their own work flows and processes.

Autonomy over one's work is a very powerful motivation tool, and an exceptional way to retain top talent. Some examples of alternative work arrangements include:

- Flextime: You schedule your work day to fit your specific work-life balance needs. This enables individuals to architect their work around outside work challenges such as family scheduling, caring for sick children/parents.
- You work your own schedule as you need, to meet a pre-set number of weekly hours all while accomplishing the goals you've set for yourself.
- Alternative work arrangements have become a widely adopted global practice, as individuals can work remotely in virtual times and remain connected to their organization through servers.

Interestingly enough, there has been a recent drawback on the work from home front, as several major corporations have begun to require that their work-from-home employees come into the office. IBM, a pioneer and champion from the work-from-home work concept is reversing a decades-long policy and calling its people back from their home offices. This is particularly surprising, as IBM has boasted that up to 40% of its entire workforce has spent work time away from traditional company offices.[88]

---

[88] John Simons, "IBM Says No to Home Work," May 19, 2017. Wall Street Journal. Page A1.

There is a belief that having employees work from home places a strain (stress) on Managers not equipped to manage employees remotely. Further, these corporations are requiring that employees come back to work, so as to make more face time available with co-workers and clients.

Understandably, work-from-home is an option that requires flexibility in adapting to each employee, should not be pursued to either extreme, and needs to be revisited on a regular basis. Compassionate organizations don't make Draconian demands of "take it or leave it!" but rather engage in an ever-evolving negotiation with their people. After all, truly enlightened organizations understand that giving their people the autonomy to architect their own work leads to happier and more productive employees.

The Many Benefits of Worker Autonomy

The benefits that organizations accrue by offering such programs include reduced absenteeism, increased productivity, reduced overtime expense, better morale, reduced lateness, and increased employee autonomy. What does worker autonomy really entail? For starters:

- Your people are closest to your clients, vendors, suppliers, the media…ALL stakeholders.
- Hire the best, give them what they need to succeed, get out of their way, and watch the MAGIC happen.
- Requires a complete culture change.
- Layers of reporting structure slow down decision-making, impede creativity & innovation, leads to top talent leaving you.

Conduct an Organizational '4T' Autonomy Audit

- One powerfully efficient and effective way to determine the degree of autonomy your organization actually grants its people is to survey them. Ask your employees on a scale of 1-10 how much/ little autonomy they have over their work in four key areas: [89]
- The *tasks* they perform; Do people have complete control over the work they perform?
- The *time* they spend on each task;

---

[89] Daniel H. Pink. Drive.

- The *teams* they get to choose to work on; and
- The *technique* they use. How they perform the various responsibilities that go into their jobs.

How much autonomy do you have over your tasks (work)	1-10
How much autonomy do you have over your time at work	1-10
How much autonomy do you have over your team (do you get to choose who you work with?)	1-10
How much autonomy do you have over your technique (how you perform the responsibilities of your job?)	1-10

Job Sharing Best Practices

Job sharing allows two or more people to share a traditional one person, 40 hour-a-week job. You can split hours worked each day, days worked each week, and the tasks required to complete a job. This is not a widely-practiced strategy, as only 12% of large companies offer it. The challenge to implementing job sharing is, there is significant difficulty finding compatible partners. A benefit of embracing is, you can leverage talents of different people to fill one job.

Telecommuting

With telecommuting, there is no commuting so employees do not waste time in transit. Further, repetitive daily commutes can have an extremely damaging long-term impact on employee "quality of life" which leads to burn out, higher absenteeism rates, and over the long-term higher levels of staff turnover. Telecommuting is an extremely attractive option for organizations to offer their employees the benefit of working from home which includes perks such as: flexible hours, the ability to dress as you want, less time commuting, fewer interruptions, more control over one's work-life balance. Typical flexible work from home solutions offer at least two days a week working from home while employees are still "connected" to their employers' office. It's a de facto 'Virtual Office.'

A recent survey of 500 companies found that 57% offer it. There are three ideal job types that are ideal for telecommuting:

1) Routine information-handling;

2) Mobile activities; and

3) Professional/knowledge-related tasks.

Benefits include larger labor pool to choose from, greater productivity, less turnover, higher morale, reduced office space costs. Drawbacks include less direct supervision, harder to coordinate teamwork, and reduce knowledge transfer.

False Assertion of Compensation as a Motivator

Until now I have not mentioned compensation as a key driver in employee motivation. That is because the research is absolutely clear, assuming employees are paid fairly for their skills and experience pay is NOT a primary driver of employee motivation.

However, it is instructive to note that the tremendous persistent imbalance in pay within organizations between Senior Management (the "C" Suite) and front-line, customer-facing staff CAN have a debilitating effect on morale and reduce motivation. People want much less inequality in organizational pay than currently exists. In a study of people in 40 countries, liberals said CEOs should be paid four times as much as the average worker. Conservatives said five times.

Let's go back to Yahoo! for an example. Marissa Mayer has been paid $293 million since she took over as CEO in 2012 after being wooed away from Google. That is more than $900,000 per week. In her time at the helm, Yahoo! was rocked by two of the biggest security breaches in U.S. history, advertisers fled its platform, users left for competitive offerings from Google, Facebook, etc. and its workforce was cut in half. The company was so weakened that its Board had little choice but to sell the company to Verizon. How can one justify her paycheck? Well, she DID make money for the company's shareholders as its stock price tripled during her tenure.[90]

Ms. Mayer is not alone in her ridiculous compensation. The average CEO at the largest American companies earns about 350 times the pay of the average worker. The data on American societal imbalance is even more staggering. The top 1% of individuals in America own more than the bottom 90%.

---

[90] "Dissecting Marissa Mayer's $900,000 a Week Paycheck." New York times. June 4, 2017. Vindu Goel.

Millennials are the first American generation that will earn LESS than their parents.[91]

I strongly suggest that Executives in organizations who control employee pay revisit the tremendous inequalities that exist in your pay structures. Inequality of all type, whether its pay, race, political views drives a wedge between employees and prevents organizations from truly becoming compassionate preferred employers and you will lose out in the pervasive war for talent.

Employee Involvement

Employee involvement or *Participative Management* entails affording employees with Joint decision-making authority shared between subordinates and their supervisors. It is a strategy to release traditional management control over people in order to empower people to take greater control over the own work.

Research has yielded mixed results in the success of employee involvement. Some benefits include higher stock returns for publicly traded companies and lower staff turnover, combined with higher levels of worker productivity. However, results are not consistently successful with many organizations experiencing only a modest increase in employee productivity.

Such uneven results indicate that this is still a relatively recent trend and much more research is required to draw meaningful results on its efficacy in unleashing employee untapped potential.

Representative Participation

Employee involvement involves a one-on-one approach between the employee and management. It The employee is included in all aspects of the decision-making process pertaining to her/his job. This process encourages an employee to take ownership of the outcome of the project they are working on. The employee affects the process itself by making decisions with management, which both encourages the employees to become more involved in the project and share their ideas on how to improve the project.

---

[91] "What Monkeys Can Teach Us About Fairness." Nicholas Kristof. New York Times. June 4, 2017.

Representative participation leads to tremendous benefits including higher employee engagement, stronger positive feelings towards the organization, more loyalty and commitment. Representative participation is a workplace strategy practiced by most countries in Western Europe. Such a strategy requires employees to be consulted when decisions affecting them are proposed by Management.

Flexible Spending Programs

Individualizes rewards by allowing each employee to choose the compensation package that best fits her current needs and situation.

- Replaces the "one benefit for all" model.

Peer Motivation

A 2014 survey by TinyHR of 500 organizations and 200,000 employees found that the #1 factor that employees cite as a motivation to drive up their performance is…the drive to see their team succeed.

Employee motivation can be achieved through either positive or negative *reinforcement*. These strategies are also referred to as the *"carrot or the stick."*

Positive reinforcement is using beneficial incentives (carrots) to boost an employee's morale and their productivity. Positive reinforcement includes such strategies as: performance based bonuses, sales commissions, recognition, achievement rewards, pay raises, and promotions. Negative reinforcement is using unfavorable tools (the stick) to achieve desired results, such as: bad performance reviews, verbal and written warnings, suspension, putting the employee on a 90-day probationary period, pay reduction or even such Draconian steps as giving them dismissal warnings contingent on having to increase performance using quantifiable metrics during the probationary period.[92]

---

[92] "Motivation & Employee Performance." http://smallbusiness.chron.com/motivation-employee-performance-1964.html. Owen E. Richason.

Opportunities for Career Growth

According to a BambooHR survey of more than 1,000 workers, a *lack of opportunities* is the single biggest factor that will chase your best employees away. [93]

As part of a Glassdoor online company review survey, employees voluntarily and anonymously shared what their job and company is like when it comes to career opportunities. Glassdoor then ranked the top 25 companies based on high career opportunities ratings and reviews about their employers. [94]

The Glassdoor's Top 5 organizations for career opportunities are:

- Bain & Co.
- Boston Consulting Group
- McKinsey & Co.
- Guidewire
- Edelman

Ways for employees and their employers to work together to create more opportunities for employee career advancement from within include:

1. Develop formal coaching & mentoring programs.
2. Learn how to quantify your performance and results using tangible proof (measured in numbers)
3. Become comfortable promoting yourself.
4. Strive to build a strong bond with your boss (also applies to bosses working harder to cultivate more meaningful relationships with their direct reports.)
5. Pursue lifelong learning and the acquisition of new skills. One way to ensure you won't get promoted or advance is to fail to keep up with the relevant industry trends and developments, and fail to maintain the highest skill level. It's a straight shot to becoming obsolete.
6. Build a powerfully robust professional network. The statement that: "It's not what you know but who you know" is true. This entails

---

[93] www.talentculture.com/what-truly-motivates-employees.

[94] www.businessinsider.com/25-best-companies-to-work-for-if-you-want-to-get-promoted-2013-10

becoming more widely known within your organization, and within your industry. A great strategy for this is to join your industry's primary professional trade association, and volunteer on one of its committees such as Membership or Programming.

7. Seek out more responsibilities. Become indispensable by expanding the depth and breadth of your involvement. Offer to work on cross-functional Teams and share your expertise.

8. Maintain the highest levels of professionalism, ethics, and values.

9. Be a Team player. I discuss this in the Team chapter.

10. Learn how to create your own opportunities. When I conduct career coaching, I always push back on clients who say they "got stuck" in a dead-end job. In fact, you have to actively work yourself into that spot. It just doesn't happen to you. [95]

Throw Away Those Performance Reviews

Instead, have your employees conduct their own personal monthly reviews of their own performance. Why? There is only marginal benefit to your people when reviews are conducted once a year. Use "Goldilocks" goals that are neither too difficult or too easy to achieve, instead of versus STRETCH goals that serve to discourage employees.

360-degree feedback is hardly ever achieved in practice. True 360-degree feedback begins with the employee giving and receiving input from a boss, peers, clients, vendors, other Departments they work with, employees they manage or lead on teams and work with in projects…everyone!

360-degree feedback takes longer to conduct, but is much more expansive and gives a much clearer picture of the employee's performance and impact on their Team and the organization. Assessment/evaluation should be conducted on a regular, ongoing basis to be of maximum value to employees.

---

[95] www.livecareer.com/quintessential/getting-promoted-strategies. "Moving Up the Ladder: 10 Strategies for Getting Yourself Promoted." Dr. Donald Wetmore.

10. Group Behavior

Why do we form groups? There are many benefits that employees gain by forming groups (work teams) within organizations.

A Sense of Kinship.

Groups provide members with a sense of belonging, that "we're all in this together." Groups enable employees to maximize their individual productivity, and gain from the collective skills, background, and experiences of people working together.

Social Identity Theory.

Individuals gain a sense of personal pride in the group's accomplishments. When a group underperforms, its members are embarrassed. People tie their own self-esteem and sense of "self-worth" to the group's performance and behavior.

Here's an exercise you and your fellow employees can do, to get an understanding of the two basic parts of **social identity theory**, as a tool to understanding how you can leverage it to increase employee motivation and thus performance.

First, think about the self-conception you have about yourself. Think about your personal skills and abilities and how they shape how you view who you are. The feeling you get when you look at who you are as it relates to these aspects and how that makes you feel about yourself. Next, take a moment to picture yourself with a group of people that have not succeeded as a team. Think about how you feel about being in that team. Picture yourself with a team or a group that has succeeded. Think about how you feel being part of a team like that.[96]

---

[96] "Social identity theory. Definition and examples." Rob Wengryzn.

The Importance of Social Identity

- Similarity: People sharing values with other members have higher affinity to the group.
- Distinctiveness: People notice characteristics how they differ from other groups.
- Status: People link themselves to high status groups.
- Uncertainty reductions: Helps you understand who you are and how you fit in the world.

The 5 Stage Model to Group Formation

Every team goes through the five stages of team development. The first four stages of team growth were first developed by Bruce Wayne Tuckman and published in 1965. His theory, called "Tuckman's Stages" was based on research he conducted on team dynamics. He believed (as is a common belief today) that these stages are inevitable in order for a team to grow to the point where they are functioning effectively together and delivering high quality results.[97]

In 1977, Tuckman, jointly with Mary Ann Jensen, added a fifth stage to the 4 stages: "Adjourning." The adjourning stage is when the team is completing the current project. They will be joining other teams and moving on to other work in the near future.

Groups go through all five key stages to achieve successful team performance. The stages are:

1 Forming: At the beginning, there is uncertainty about group's purpose, structure, and its leadership.

- The "forming" stage takes place when the team first meets each other. In this first meeting, team members are introduced to each. They share information about their backgrounds, interests and experience and form first impressions of each other. They learn about the project they will be working on, discuss the project's objectives/goals and start to think about what role they will play

---

[97] www.projectsmart.co.uk/the-five-stages-of-team-development-a-case-study.php

on the project team. They are not yet working on the project. They are, effectively, "feeling each other out" and finding their way around how they might work together.

- During this initial stage of team growth, it is important for the team leader to be very clear about team goals and provide clear direction regarding the project. The team leader should ensure that all of the members are involved in determining team roles and responsibilities and should work with the team to help them establish how they will work together ("team norms"). The team is dependent on the team leader to guide them.

2 Storming: Intragroup conflict arises between members as they accept the group but resist its constraints.

- As the team begins to work together, they move into the "storming" stage. This stage is not avoidable; every team - most especially a new team who has never worked together before - goes through this part of developing as a team. In this stage, the team members compete with each other for status and for acceptance of their ideas. They have different opinions on what should be done and how it should be done - which causes conflict within the team. As they go progress through this stage, with the guidance of the team leader, they learn how to solve problems together, function both independently and together as a team, and settle into roles and responsibilities on the team. For team members who do not like conflict, this is a difficult stage to go through.

- The team leader needs to be adept at facilitating the team through this stage - ensuring the team members learn to listen to each other and respect their differences and ideas. This includes not allowing any one team member to control all conversations and to facilitate contributions from all members of the team. The team leader will need to coach some team members to be more assertive and other team members on how to be more effective listeners.

3 Norming: Close relationships begin to form as the group comes together with the shared sense of mission and purpose.

- When the team moves into the "norming" stage, they are beginning to work more effectively as a team. They are no longer focused on their individual goals, but rather are focused on developing a way of working together (processes and procedures). They respect each other's opinions and value their differences. They begin to see the value in those differences on the team.

- Working together as a team seems more natural. In this stage, the team has agreed on their team rules for working together, how they will share information and resolve team conflict, and what tools and processes they will use to get the job done. The team members begin to trust each other and actively seek each other out for assistance and input. Rather than compete against each other, they are now helping each other to work toward a common goal. The team members also start to make significant progress on the project as they begin working together more effectively.

4 Performing: The group focuses on its goals, mission, and tasks it needs to complete.

- In the "performing" stage, teams are functioning at a very high level. The focus is on reaching the goal as a group. The team members have gotten to know each other, trust each other and rely on each other.

- Not every team makes it to this level of team growth; some teams stop at Stage 3: Norming. The highly performing team functions without oversight and the members have become interdependent. The team is highly motivated to get the job done. They can make decisions and problem solve quickly and effectively.

- When they disagree, the team members can work through it and come to consensus without interrupting the project's progress. If there needs to be a change in team processes - the team will come to agreement on changing processes on their own without reliance on the team leader.

5 Adjourning: Members complete the tasks they were faced with, and prepare to disband and move onto new Teams and new projects.

- In the "adjourning" stage the project is coming to an end and the team members prepare to move on to different directions by joining other project teams.

- The team leader should ensure that there is time for the team to celebrate the success of the project, and capture the best practices used to put into future use. Or, if it was not a successful project, then use the lessons learned to evaluate what happened and capture ways the team could have acted differently for a more positive outcome in future projects. Adjourning provides the team with the opportunity to say good-bye to each other and wish each other luck as they pursue their next endeavor. It is likely that any group that reached Stage 4: Performing will keep in touch with each other as they have become a very close-knit group and there will be sadness at separating from the positive experience and moving on to other projects.

<u>Roles</u>

- All group members are actors playing a role which is a set of behavior patterns attributed to the position you occupy within the group.
- Work-life balance roles can be complicated because we all play a number of roles both at work and in our personal lives. Meaning we may play dominant roles at work, and more submissive at home, or vice versa.
- *Role perception*: OUR view of how we are supposed to act in a given situation.
- *Role expectations*: The way OTHERS believe that you should act in a given situation.

8 Roles Employees Play and Group Behaviors

There are two key terms that require understanding as applies to the roles that employees play within groups and the behaviors of groups:

- Psychological contract - An unwritten agreement between employees and an employer defining mutual expectations for the work that employees must perform.
- Role conflict - Complying with one role requirement makes it difficult to comply with others.

1. Norms

All groups have norms, the acceptable standards of behavior that members follow. The Hawthorne Studies at Western Electric Co. studied work environments and productivity and discovered people's performance influenced by status of being special, and people don't individually maximize their productivity but tied to the group's work norms.

2. Conformity

Individuals conform to the behavior of the group, in order to be accepted. Under conformity, groups can pressure its members to change their personal attitudes and behaviors to meet the group's standards. This is called "PEER PRESSURE" and it can have a significant effect on individuals conforming to the group.

Deviant Workplace Behaviors Threaten Morale

Compassionate organizations understand that unacceptable employee behavior can have damaging effects on a group's performance and the organization's culture. These anti-social behaviors serve to undermine the group's ability to achieve its short and long-term goals by allowing dysfunction between employees to exist.

Such behavior is also referred to as *workplace incivility* or *antisocial behavior*. It is voluntary behavior that employees initiate that violates their organization's accepted norms, that can threaten the well -being of the organization and its employees. Through my consulting working with both for-profits and non-profits I have found that despite employers denying it exists in their organizations, it often does.

Such behavior entails a rudeness and disregard towards others by bosses and co-workers. The range of behaviors encompass general anti-social behaviors and when taken to the extreme can lead to harassment.

It often helps to have an outside behavioral psychologist conduct and interpersonal audit by reviewing formal written/field grievances between employees, and documented cases of social dysfunction. Often a pervasive, organization-wide issue stems from top-down tolerance. An extremely public example of this is the culture of misogyny and sexual abuse that exists at Uber.

4-P Model of Deviant Behavior

- Production: Wasting resources, working slowly, leaving early.
- Property: Sabotage, lying about hours worked, pilfering (5 Finger Discount.)
- Political: Showing favoritism, gossiping, spreading rumors, blaming co-workers.
- Personal aggression: Sexual, physical harassment, verbal abuse, stealing from co-workers.

Organizational Citizenship Behavior

"Organizational citizenship behavior (OCB) is defined as behavior that (a) goes beyond the basic requirements of the job, (b) is to a large extent discretionary, and (c) is of benefit to the organization" (Lambert, S.J., 2006, p. 503-525). "OCBs are employee behaviors that, although not critical to the task or job, serve to facilitate organizational functioning" (Lee and Allen, 2002, p 132)[98]

3. Status

Status is defined as a socially defined position or rank given to groups/ members BY OTHERS. Status within organizations accrue from lengthy

---

[98] https://workfamily.sas.upenn.edu/glossary/o/organizational-citizenship-behavior-definitions.

service for an organization, a significant amount of general or specific subject matter expertise that others rely on, or a politically savvy individual who understands how to successfully navigate the political landscape within their organizational to achieve desired outcomes.

Status also pertains to the social connections that an individual possesses with others who are in positions of power thus the power extends to that individual through their relationships.

An example would be the "Untouchables" caste system that exists in India. Status is determined by the power that people have over each other, one's ability to contribute to the success of the group(s) they work in, and the individual's personal characteristics.

4. Size of the Group

German sociologist Georg Simmel argued that as the group becomes greater, the individual becomes separated and grows more alone, isolated and segmented. Clearly then, the size of the group affects people's behavior within the group. It is important to understand that within such group dynamics, other factors also affect behavior. Following are the functions that can be best performed by size of group as well as the emotions/affects achieved by participating in these size groups:[99]

Group Size	Task Function	Affective Functions
Individuals	Personal reflection: - generating personal data	Personal focus increases 'safety': - personal focus means positive start - brings a sense of belonging and ownership

---

[99] "Group dynamics. How group size affects function." www.faculty.londondeanery. ac.uk/e-learning/small-group-teaching/group-dynamics-how-group-size-affects-function.

Pairs/three	Generating data: - checking out data - sharing interpretations - good for basic communication skills practice (e.g. listening, questioning, clarifying) - good size for co-operative working.	Builds sense of safety: - builds sense of confidence by active involvement (self-belief) - lays foundation for sharing and co-operating in bigger group - reticent members can still take part
Four to ten	Generating ideas: - criticizing ideas - usually sufficient numbers to enable allocation of roles and responsibilities, therefore wide range of work can be tackled (ex. project work, problem-based learning)	Decreasing safety for reticent members: - at lower end of the range still difficult for members to 'hide', this risk increases with size - strong can still enthuse the weak - size of group still small enough to avoid splintering - sufficient resources to enable creative support
10+	Holding on to a task focus becomes difficult: - size hinders discussion but workshop activities possible, e.g. using purposeful sub-groups to address some of the issues	Difficulties in maintaining supportive climate: - 'hiding' becomes common - 'dominance' temptation and leadership struggles a risk - divisive possibilities with spontaneous splintering into sub-groups

EXAMPLES?

Social loafing occurs when individuals take advantage of a group dynamic by failing to performance at a high level. The central concept of maximizing group performance is that the aggregate total group performance increases as the group size increases. It is instructive to note that average worker productivity diminishes with the addition of new members.

WHY???

An example of this is in the military, when groups that saw its ranks diminished due to deaths in battle dealt with adding replacement soldiers who had to be meshed into the fold and be productive after the remaining members had already forged powerful individual relationships.

5. Cohesiveness Within the Group

Cohesiveness is the degree to which members are attracted to and stay committed to one another. It has a direct impact on the group's productivity. Steps that you can implement, in order to make your group more cohesive include:

- Make the group smaller;
- Develop group-based goals;
- Increase the time group members spend together;
- Increase the group's status within your organization;
- Create competition with other groups;
- Give out group rewards during reward & recognition ceremonies; and
- Isolate the group to create a member sense of shared exclusivity.

6. Diversity

The composition of a team is a very important factor in determining how the Team performs together. Research is absolutely consistent in that he greater the true diversity of the group, the stronger thee performance.

- Surface level: Cultural, racial, gender, background, age, tenure.
- Deep level: Attitudes, values, beliefs.
- Studies of MBA students show surface level diversity influences students to be MORE open-minded.
- Diversity in groups shows mixed results.
- Fault lines: side effect of diverse teams esp. in surface level factors split groups into sub-groups that are harmful to group functioning.

See the Chapter on Diversity & Inclusion for a comprehensive analysis of Diversity.

7. Group Think

A group phenomenon in which members attempt to get others to join into the beliefs, position, or ideas help by a majority of the group. An interesting phenomenon of group behavior in group think is when individuals make excuses when we face resistance to our own assumptions. Members try to influence other members who doubt the group's consensus. Dissenting members tend to keep quiet in order to remain a part of the group and be accepted as a member in "good standing."

A dangerous potential outcome of group think is that there can often be a false appearance of a unanimous voice as dissenting viewpoints are silenced. Conflict in group dynamics is often a positive outcome, as long as the conflict can be maintained with civility so that opposing viewpoints are allowed to "battle" for the greatest good of the group.

The free expression of group-based dissenting viewpoints is the underpinning of the Socratic Method and one of the most powerful tools to achieving true group-based learning by challenging the broadest range of often opposing viewpoints, ideas.

The Socratic Method for Team-Building

Using the Socratic Method in team-based discussion to solve problems and thinking critically you have someone take a position on a controversial issue the team is struggling with. Someone on the Team asks a question to make that person explain themselves.

Other Team members are then free to ask a follow up question/questions, in order to exploit a potential weakness of the answer to the first question. You keep going, until the Team either establishes or disproves the person's argument.

8. Group Shift

Under Group Shift, the group's decision reflects the collective decision of the most powerful/dominant sub-group (the power brokers) within the larger group. Within groups, a shift towards group polarization or sub-groups taking opposing viewpoints often reflects the success of the group as a whole, as it indicates that group members are more comfortable enough in group to express their extreme views.

One behavior that is interesting to note within group shift is when individuals on the fringes or the outside express extreme views, with the intent of emphasizing their own unique values and beliefs especially when they feel their voice is not being heard.

Reward & Recognition

R&R programs reward and recognize employees for achieving outstanding performance, and for achieving goals that are in alignment with team and organization-wide goals. The only limit to R&R programs is the creativity of the organization. Here are some very creative ideas for motivational R&R programs.

- **Queen or King for the Quarter.** Dayton Metro Housing created the QUEST employee recognition program to improve employee motivation and reward their workforce for demonstrating good customer service skills. Each quarter, employees receive three tokens. When they spot a fellow employee or manager providing good customer service, they hand them a QUEST token. At the end of the quarter, the person with the highest number of tokens is crowned king or queen. Those with eight or more tokens are "knighted." All the King, Queens, and Knights attend a special banquet. At the end of the year all token winners can use their tokens to bid on various awards and prizes. Furthermore, the individual with the highest yearly number of tokens is bequeathed a "scepter."
- **You're Magnificent!** At MAG Insurance Co. they use a form of peer recognition called "You're Magnificent!" The form is printed in triplicate and given to all employees to nominate each other for outstanding behavior. The top copy goes to the recognized employee. The second copy goes to the employee's supervisor. The third copy is posted for everyone to see on a bulletin board. Once a month they take the posted copies and randomly draw the

names of five individuals called, "You're Magnificents" for $10 gift certificates. Then three additional "Magnificents" are drawn each quarter for a $250 gift certificate.

- **Safety Bingo**. For every accident-free day at the Emory Conference Center Hotel, associates are awarded a bingo number. Each associate has a card and plays the game. A pot grows at the rate of $1 per day with a starting amount of $100. The associate who wins at safety bingo is awarded the cash in the pot. If they go over 100 days without an accident, it increases by $2 per day. If we have an accident, the pot falls back down to $100 and it starts over again. If someone wins, the pot remains at same pay out level, and continues to grow $1 or $2 per day. This program reduced accidents by 50% each year.[100]

Collaboration.

The future of work is sharing. We are now in the era of ***workplace collaboration and collaborative communities***, the Open Source Movement.

The days of hoarding information, developing proprietary intellectual capital that is selfishly held under organizational "lock and key" is so…20th Century. In today's era of Big Data, mobile processing, cloud computing and virtual work teams, organizations that embrace collaboration gain lasting competitive advantage.

Successful organizations understand that in order to maintain their competitive advantage, they have no choice but to collaborate their way to lasting success.

Steve Jobs Inspired a Collaboration Culture at Pixar

Steve Jobs famously redesigned the offices at Pixar, which originally housed computer scientists in one building, animators in a second building, and executives and editors in a third. Jobs recognized that separating these groups, each with its own culture and approach to problem-solving, discouraged them from sharing ideas and solutions.[101]

---

[100] www.chartcourse.com/motivating-employees-for-high-performance.
[101] http://99u.com/articles/16408/how-to-build-a-collaborative-office-space-like-pixar-and-google.

Perhaps the animators could introduce a fresh perspective when the computer scientists became stuck; and maybe the executives would learn more about the nuts and bolts of the business if they occasionally met an animator in the office kitchen, or a computer scientist at the water cooler. Jobs ultimately succeeded in creating a single cavernous office that housed the entire Pixar team, and John Lasseter, Pixar's chief creative officer, declared that he'd "never seen a building that promoted collaboration and creativity as well as this one."

These days, even business competitors are forced to work together... "**co-opetition**" between such traditional adversaries as Google, Microsoft, Apple...is the new normal. An excellent example of co-opetition in practice was when Samsung and Sony's successfully collaborated in 2006 to jointly produce LCD screens. **Co-opetition really is all about the following: "If you can't beat 'em, join 'em!"**

These firms have found a way to work with one another in certain industries, evolving technologies and new product ideas, and yet still compete in other areas. Organizations that truly understand the power of sharing and collaboration encourage their people to share.

For Inspiration, Consider Linux.

The computer operating system Linux powers 98% of the world's supercomputers, most of the servers that keep the Internet humming, and tens of millions of Android mobile phones and gadgets. As an open-source system, Linux relies on the collaboration of programmers from around the world.[102]

And of Course, There's Collaboration Firm...Google.

Google encourages its people to collaborate within and across teams by aligning Objectives & Key Results (OKRs) developed by ***John Doerr***. If OKRs are done well when they are (1) connected to top line company goals (2) shared openly- so anyone can see anyone's goals and why it matters to the company and (3) cross-functionally aligned so dependencies across teams are clear from the get go as part of planning process.

Wikipedia has achieved such wide scale success as a platform driven by mass user content contributions where people freely share their own intellectual

---

[102] Chad Caydo. "Lessons From Linux: How to Foster Collaboration at Meetings and Conferences."

capital. In the 20th Century, organizations that controlled the platforms to disseminate information (the media) controlled the message and the very nature of conversation. Today's sharing organizations facilitate the free flow of information to enable the sharing of ideas by enabling individuals talk to the world via the Internet and social media.

We can now collaborate online, work productively in virtual teams with members all over the world, and disseminate radical, even revolutionary ideas that spark movements to change the world like the Arab Spring and Occupy Wall Street.

Organizations that dominate their respective industries are the ones that most effectively leverage their people's talents and unleash their employees' full, untapped potential. They do this by developing learning organizations where they coach and train their people to use creativity and innovation in project-driven teams. They foster friendly competitions within their organizations and within their industry through professional associations.

TAKE-AWAY: How does your organization foster workplace sharing and collaboration to create a learning organization?

11. The Sharing Economy

By definition, the sharing economy, which evolved in response to the 2007-2009 recession and was fueled by the Internet, opens up opportunities for people to work for themselves on a full-time basis or make extra money on the side.

A definition:

Investopedia defines the sharing economy as an economic model in which individuals are able to buy or rent assets owned by somebody else, a practice that has become easier with the rise of the Internet.[103]

Built on the idea of peer-to-peer exchanges to buy/sell/rent personal items or services, the sharing economy is a platform that provides access to items or services (sometimes for a set period of time) so users don't have to purchase them. The online landscape is bursting with buyer-seller communities of **'collaborative consumption'**, where people list items they wish to rent out or borrow such as bicycles, cars, apartments or parking spaces.[104]

It All Began with an Airbed

The boom in the sharing economy began in 2008 when Brian Chesky and Joe Gebbia decided to offer a place to sleep (on an air bed on their floor) in their San Francisco apartment to people attending an industrial design conference. Initially done to earn some fast cash to pay the bills, the venture proved popular. Shortly after, Chesky and Gebbia set up a dedicated domain, Airbnb, allowing people from all over the world to offer accommodations in their living quarters for an affordable fee.

Since then, more than 50 million people have used the site as a means of finding accommodations. Many sharing businesses have popped up since Airbnb, all of which respond to and facilitate the demand of paying for what you use on an as-needed basis.

[103] http://kwhs.wharton.upenn.edu/2017/03/5-truths-sharing-economy/
[104] Mine, Yours, Ours: The Sharing Economy. Anna Rees. RESET.

The key driving force behind the sharing economy is perceived value. Price-conscious customers search for less costly alternatives to items offered in a retail market. Thus, the sharing economy began to soar during the financial crisis of 2008. Some sharing venues are free (like Couchsurfing where travelers can stay on a host's couch for free) while others are based on financial transactions, like Airbnb. The advent and proliferation of technology has made it easier to provide or seek goods to share or rent that are cheaper and quicker than ever before.

How the Sharing Economy Affects Work

In his Forbes article entitled Are Uber, Airbnb And Other Sharing Economy Businesses Good for America? Jacob Morgan asks us to "Imagine a world where there are no employees. Instead everyone is an independent worker that moves around from company to company, project to project, and task to task. This is what most of the media and business publications are making it seem the future will look like, and they are wrong.

While we will indeed see the trend towards independent workers increase, this trend will by no means reach the exorbitantly large levels that some are reporting. Still, it is true that we no longer need to rely on organizations as our only source of income. Today you can drive for Uber or Lyft, rent out your place on Airbnb, sell products directly on Etsy, or offer your services on Upwork."

Morgan is right in observing that there has been a significant increase in the number of independent workers who either choose to seek freelance, independent work gigs because it fits their lifestyle or they are forced into such work gigs because they are underemployed or lack full-time work options.

He continues: "The sharing economy, in simplest terms, is "an economic model in which individuals are able to borrow or rent assets owned by someone else[3]." While there have always been collaborative economies involving shared purchases or the shared use of goods (think coops and thrift stores), what enables the explosive growth of the sharing economy today is the internet. Barriers to sharing (time, space, geography, marketing dollars) are rendered irrelevant in the digital age of free mobile apps that connect people across time zones, cultures, and languages. Of course, we should also mention Freelance marketplaces like Upwork and Work Market, which are part of the sharing ecosystem but are focused more on services instead of just on assets.'"

From a survey by PwC and BAV Consulting entitled: <u>The Sharing Economy Consumer Intelligence Series</u> "Around the world, a new wave of peer-to-peer, access-driven businesses are shaking up established categories. Whether borrowing goods, renting homes, or serving up micro-skills in exchange for access or money, consumers are showing a robust appetite for the sharing-based economy."

- 44% of US consumers are familiar with the sharing economy;
- 19% of the total US adult population has engaged in a sharing economy transaction;
- 57% agree "I am intrigued by companies in the sharing economy but have some concerns about them"; and
- 72% agree "I could see myself being a consumer in the sharing economy in the next two years."

How (Does) The Sharing Economy Impact Traditional Work?

There is the distinct danger of overstating the case and the size of the effects of the sharing economy on traditional work. A 2014 paper by Annette Bernhardt of UC Berkeley, signals a cautionary note about any claims of radical recent change being wrought across the U.S. economy:

>*[We] all share a strong intuition that the nature of work has fundamentally changed, contributing to the deterioration of labor standards. Yet at least with aggregate national data, it has been hard to find evidence of a strong, unambiguous shift toward nonstandard or contingent forms of work – especially in contrast to the dramatic increase in wage inequality. This is not to say that there have been no changes in the workplace. But as this paper has emphasized, for enforcement agencies and policymakers, it may be more fruitful to focus on specific industries and regions in assessing when and where pernicious forms of nonstandard work have grown, and which groups of workers have been most impacted.*

It is true that the rise of independent workers, and associated job insecurity, long predates the recent rise of the sharing economy, although their percentage of all U.S. workers is expected to grow from about one-third currently to 40% by 2020, according to some estimates.[105]

The bottom line is, the sharing economy is driven by many factors. Independent workers who seek to supplement their existing income may do so if they are already working, or as a means of earning a viable alternate source of income in the case that they are underemployed or cannot find full-time work. Additional research needs to be conducted to determine the root causes why people are engaged in independent work roles rather than full-time employment.

The Gig Economy and Alternative Workforce

A Perma-Temp New Work Order?

A fundamental question that begs asking is: "What does it mean to be an employee in the gig, tech-enabled, and service-driven 21st century American economy? Are we talking about an "on-demand" many serving the privileged few?

In other words, is an economy based on an ever-growing army of contract workers good or bad for employees? The answer is not so simple, and depends on what kind of worker we're talking about.

From a study conducted by Rand in 2015 of 4,000 workers, nearly all new jobs growth in America between 2005 and 2015 can be attributed to alternate work.

The research uncovered showed that 84% of independent workers want to work for themselves, yet 80% are concerned about the volatility of their income and the lack of benefits they receive. However, 77% of America's 16 million American temporary workers would prefer full-time jobs.

Temporary workers are afforded more legal protections, but they make less per hour then permanent employees. They often do not receive sick days,

---

[105] "Uber, Airbnb and consequences of the sharing economy: Research roundup." Joanna Penn, John Wihbey.

vacation, insurance, retirement plan, and often little in the way of safety training.

The ugly side of contract work with so many intermediary providers.

- The recession has forced millions of Americans into lower paying jobs;
- The National Employment Law Project says there are 1.2 million fewer jobs in the mid-to-high wage industries than before the Recession and 2.3 million more jobs in lower wage sectors;
- The gig economy is a STOP-GAP solution for workers who cannot make ends meet in a weak labor market.

Organizational loop holes to avoid labor laws.

When taken to the extreme, organizations can and have intentionally mis-classified workers in order to significantly lower worker pay rates which has led to many class action lawsuits. In response, some companies have responded by moving away from contract workers in order to avoid such lawsuits.

The challenge with traditional employment was, there were only two "buckets" of worker. Full-time employees and contractors. Given the lines of worker have blurred in the gig economy, the time has come for a new classification of worker, a third "Other" category requiring a new legal classification of intermediaries. Perhaps we call this new third option of employee an independent contractor and afford them rights along the lines of permanent employees.

According to U.S. Labor Dept. Wage and Hour Division Head David Weil, the American labor department has to play "catch up" by offering more buckets of employee category afforded certain protections. Without such intervention, we can continue to see a more fractured workplace in which companies wash their hands of labor laws by engaging contract workers and take the approach: "Not our employees…not our problem."

Elizabeth Warren has proposed possible solutions to the pitfalls inherent in a gig economy:

State run portable insurance plans or contract workers/freelancers run by a union or other organization and contracted invested management to the private sector. Expand social security to include temporary employees. Offer healthcare benefits to temporary employees through expanded Medicaid and health care exchanges. One option is to increase regulation and clarify laws around part-time work. Provide universal right for contract workers to organize.

In the meantime, the Obama and Trump Administrations have been telling us there has been a steady rise in America's post-recession employment figures. But the research actually shows that from 2005-2015 total employment increased by 9.1 million jobs. Of those newly created jobs, gig-based jobs increased by 9.4 million according to the U.S. Department of Labor.

A Freelancers Union 2015 study entitled: "Freelancing in America 2015" revealed that 54 million U.S. workers do at least some freelance work and represent approximately one third of the U.S. work force. According to Freelancers Union Founder Sarah Horowitz "freelancing is the new normal" of work in America.

A workforce without rights or power.

So why does this matter (esp. to Millennials) and what are the long-term implications for workers? According to Robert Reich, there are many concerns about how the changing nature of work will adversely affect employees who are forced to exist relying on "on-demand work."

The change in work from full-time to alternative gig shifts all economic risks onto the worker.

It also eliminates all labor protections for employees such as minimum wage, O/T pay, medical leave, and worker safety protections. It even weds employer-financed insurance like social security workers compensation, unemployment benefits, and employer-provided health insurance.

Developing a more equitable worker-employer contract

We are at the point where the idea of work, employee, and employee-employer contract need to be revisited to reflect our transforming workplace. Some solutions to consider as we move forward:

- A *blended* workforce that maximizes full-time, alternative and hybrid worker options.

- Rely more on your organization's existing incumbent workforce for recruiting new workers.
- Offer more benefits to alternative workers.
- Re-imagine the role of a full-time employee and structure full-time work differently.

12. Innovation & Creativity

Innovation is the lifeblood to any organization's continued success. It helps overcome the many challenges we face. Here's why:

Organizations face challenges EVERYWHERE, from global competition to rapid changes in technology, changing demographics, an aging population, etc. Too big to fail is no longer a realistic survival reality. Huge organizations are becoming extinct at a faster rate of attrition than ever before. Here's the proof. In 1958, the average life span of an S&P 500 company was 58 years. Today **it's less than 18 years.**

> "The success of corporate R&D is on every C-suite agenda. Yet wide disparities persist in how well innovation investments actually pay off. As a consequence, R&D is often seen as a black box, where large sums of money go in and innovative products and services only sometimes come out."
> **Global Innovation 1000**

We need to infuse our organizations with a creative spirit, by empowering its people to embrace innovation.

So…What is "Creativity" anyway? Why bother pursuing it for your organization?

Creativity means looking at the same information as everyone else, and seeing something different.

Okay, but what is 'Innovation' and why is THAT a mission-critical imperative for your future success?

Innovation entails turning creative ideas into action. It's all about what's NEW, BETTER, NEXT.

So, why is innovation so critical to your organization's future survival?

Organizations face challenges are everywhere, from global competition, a persistent increase in the rate of technological innovation, changing demographics/population characteristics, an aging population, etc. The PERVASIVENESS of software demands that organizations and their employees constantly pursue innovation and a survival imperative.

China's rise as THE global innovation powerhouse is forcing other nations to adapt and respond QUICKLY. Too big to fail is no longer a valid protection against seismic industrial change. As a gauge for the rapid change of transformation driving our need for innovation, in 1958 the average life span of an S&P 500 company was 58 years. Today, it is less than 18 years.

Following are actionable steps that you can take NOW, to foster a culture of innovation within your organization.

Have a mission that truly matters, that inspires others by making emotional connections with them.

You need to plan…and PLAN TO FAIL. Innovative organizations don't just happen. You need to plan for it. It is crucial that you understand that innovation entails trial and error. Therefore, you need to not only to be willing to FAIL, but to see failure as exploration and success, NOT as failure. This is often difficult to accomplish when your organization invests significant time, effort, and resources you would normally invest in current operations, products, and services.

The critical imperative of seeing continual innovation as an ongoing pursuit, and not a destination to be reached. Create an IDEA GENERATION program for your organization and include everyone. Set aside a cross-functional team to meet on a recurring regular basis to review all ideas that you actively solicit from all of your people, and decide which ideas will be funded/pursued based on their ability to help you achieve your short and long-term business objectives.

You MUST have an organizational passion for innovation ideally championed by your CEO and constantly pursued by your Senior Management Team.

The positive is that MANY organizations have already embraced innovation, and have set the lead for other organizations to serve as proof of what it takes to be GREAT at it.

Examples of Innovation-Driven Organizations.

1. Google has created a culture of creativity entitled the "**8 Pillars of Innovation.**" The company actively promotes/embraces **BLUE SKY** thinking, where employees are encouraged to pursue the wildest ideas without any regard to limitations or practical constraints. To build and maintain this Innovation-driven culture, Google allows its employees to dedicate **20%** of their time on innovation, by giving them *INNOVATION TIME OFF*.

Would your organization consider doing that? If the answer is "YES!" then great, you have a culture of innovation. If NOT…you need to be the Agent of Change that is needed in your own organization to convince your senior management to implement an Innovation-driven culture.

2. Adobe offers a KICKBOX campaign in which it gives its employees a box filled with creativity tools including a $1,000 prepaid credit card to spend on any new innovative pursuits.

3. An Amazon key principle is "Invent and Simplify." They embrace this principle and actively promote it throughout the company.

4. Intuit has a CEO Leadership award that is gives out to executives who help to create start-ups inside the company.

How can you and your employees become truly innovative in everything you do?

It helps to know that there are no silver bullets or magic lists to follow. Only environments where innovation is MORE likely to occur. By developing a culture that fosters creativity and innovation, you will be more likely to BE innovative. Sound simple…? It will help you to always talk to and observe your customers, with a singular focus on solving their problems:

Dan Buchner who was the head of Proctor & Gamble's product development team had his team spend time in customer homes watching them, which led to the development of the Swiffer product line.

Record all of your ideas and thoughts about problems. You need to be diligent in tracking all of your inspirations and committing them to writing.

Don't think "REPRODUCTIVELY".

Most people settle on the most promising approach based on our past experiences and we tend to exclude other options as we work within a clearly defined direction towards the solution. BREAK THIS PATTERN OF BEHAVIOR! (From an interview with Michael Michalko.) You and your Team can cultivate your collective creativity by implementing the following 2 approaches:

(a) Constantly try to improve your idea, product, service. This is important because your early ideas are usually not true (your best) ideas as they are only partially formed "baked"; and

(b) Challenge your assumptions – To test an assumption, reverse it and try to make the reverse work.

1. Sketch your ideas: 99U talk from Twitter creator Jack Dorsey.
2. Use "lateral thinking skills" as Paul Sloane, visionary creativity problem-solver notes this entails looking at things in an entirely NEW way.
3. Employ "wrong thinking."
4. Mix different ideas together to see what new and interesting combinations arise as outcomes.
5. Follow *Einstein's EIGHT-step* **SCAMPER** process to improve a system, process, product or idea:

You can and should re-frame the challenge you face, by looking at it in another way. Here's how:

1. Ask powerful questions.
2. Challenge your assumptions.
3. Foster multiple perspectives.

Change the parameters you are faced with:

Think of a parameter in your market as being different then it currently is today. Next, imagine the products/services that would best serve that different reality. This gets you thinking down a different path. Some examples how you can change the parameters of the situation you find yourself confronting to change your reality:

(a) Ex. A vehicle currently requires a driver to navigate it. Imagine removing that requirement altogether, and you are left with a vehicle that DRIVES ITSELF. (Hello, Google!)

(b) Ex. How might you design a store IF…you were able to identify exactly who each visitor/patron was and all of their past purchase behavior as soon as they entered?

- Solve a PARADOX: Ex. Apple set out to get a bigger screen for its iPhone by reducing the size of the device.
- Find CONNECTIONS: Orville and Wilbur Wright watched birds in flight, in order to better understand and ultimately solve manned flight.
- Elevate "ASKING QUESTIONS" to an art form.

Experiment: Gain invaluable experience by watching, and/or making something yourself. This entails "tinkering." Follow your natural curiosity as far as you possibly can.

- Instead of taking a PROBLEM -SOLUTION approach, use a SOLUTION-PROBLEM approach. This means you find a solution first, then go in search of problems the new solution addresses.
- Use the following five step process:

(a) Define your problem clearly.

(b) Throw out any constraints.

(c) Ensure that those people working with you to solve a problem are passionate.

(d) Ideate in small teams: Known as the "Design thinking process." Jeff Bezos at Amazon feels it should only take 2 pizzas to feed a team. Keep the team SMALL to maximize the likelihood of a successful team working experience.

(e) Have competitions and give prizes for the best innovation.

1. Measure your learning, NOT the outcomes achieved. Ex. You want to keep track of the number of customers that you interviewed, NOT your results.

Ask powerfully enlightening questions such as:

(i) What did you/we learn?

(ii) What don't we still know?

(iii) What are the limits to the metrics that we are using?

You get what you measure!

In their book "The Alchemy of Growth" *Mehrdad Baghai and Stephen Coley* outlined a three-horizon model that lays out an excellent map of how to proceed.[106]

Horizon 1 - Sustaining innovation: entails investing in established products and services to maximize sales and revenue streams from your existing business. Examples of this approach include adding new products to your existing list of offerings, rolling out new product features on existing products, additional service offerings, pursuing a store expansion strategy, etc.

Horizon 2 - Adjacent innovation: Ex. Mercedes develops electric fuel vehicles. The market is experiencing rapid growth, and Mercedes does NOT want to get "left behind." and;

Horizon 3 - Disruptive innovation: Mercedes Benz invests in Car2Go, allowing customers to "rent" a Mercedes Benz where ever they are to travel very short distances. This is ideal for major metropolitan areas for target segments with extremely high disposable income.

4. Resources for you to evaluate/consider and perhaps use in your own Innovation & Creativity pursuits:

1. www.innovationinpractice.com
2. Clay Christensen, "The innovator's dilemma." DISRUPTIVE innovation versus sustaining innovation.
3. Stephen Johnson, "Where good ideas come from."
4. Scott Anthony, "The little black book of innovation."
5. Michael Michalko, "Thinker toys: A handbook of business creativity."
6. Linda Hill, "Collective genius: the art and practice of leading innovation."
7. The PWC Global Innovation 1000 Research Study

---

[106] www.movestheneedle.com/whatis-innovation

13. Sustainability

What is sustainability?

Many U.S. companies are still woefully ignorant of, and failing to respond to many sustainability challenges like climate change and resource scarcities. Ceres, a non-profit that studies sustainability has found several companies that are leading the way towards sustainability-focused cultures.

Why Does It Matter to Employees?

Employees at semiconductor-chip-maker Intel recently devised a new chemistry process that reduced chemical waste by 900,000 gallons, saving $45 million annually. Another team developed a plan to reuse and optimize networking systems in offices, which cut energy costs by $22 million. [107]

The projects produced financial and environmental benefits, of course. But just as valuable is the company's ability to energize and empower front-line employees. New data shows that sustainability is an increasingly important factor in attracting and managing talent.

Bain & Company recently surveyed about 750 employees across industries in Brazil, China, India, Germany, the UK, and the U.S. Roughly two-thirds of respondents said they care more about sustainability now than three years ago, with almost that many saying sustainable business is extremely important to them. Interest peaks among employees age 36 to 40 — a young group but not the youngest.

Employees expect employers to step up and nurture this growing interest. When asked which group should take the lead on sustainability, more respondents cited employers than they did consumers, employees, governments, or all equally. In the developed world, a small but growing segment of what we call "sustainability enthusiasts" view sustainability as a major factor in job choices

---

[107] https://hbr.org. "Sustainability matters in the Battle for Talent." Jenny Davis-Peccound. May 20, 2013.

and are willing to accept lower compensation to work for an employer that meshes with their beliefs.

They also want to be involved in developing sustainability strategy. Half of younger employees, about one-fifth of older employees and three-quarters of enthusiasts expect to play a role in how their firms approach the topic. And in a departure from attitudes five or 10 years ago, most employees care more about ensuring that the business operations themselves are sustainable than they do about philanthropic activities, as shown in this chart.

Examples

Some examples of corporations that are exhibiting a compassionate culture focus on sustainability-related causes include:

- Alcoa: one fifth of all its executive cash compensation is tied to safety, diversity and environmental stewardship, which includes greenhouse gas emission reductions and energy efficiency.
- PepsiCo: presents its sustainability strategy and goals during its annual shareholder meeting and identifies and discloses climate change, water scarcity and public health issues as core sustainability challenges in its annual financial filings.
- GE: uses its human resource dept. to integrate sustainability into the company's culture, ranging from hiring practices and training to employee wellbeing programs.
- Adobe: aims to achieve a 75% reduction, from 2000 levels, in company emissions by 2015. It is using renewable energy technologies, including hydrogen fuel cells and solar arrays, and is also focused on reducing energy needs by improving the cooling efficiency of its data centers and "virtualizing" many of its systems, platforms and devices.

- Dell: integrates alternative, recycled and recyclable materials in its product and packaging design, improvements in energy efficiency, and design for end-of-life and recyclability. One of the company's commitments is to reduce the energy intensity of its product portfolio by 80% by 2020. [108]

---

[108] www.theguardian.com/sustainable-business/blog/best-practices-sustainability-us-corporations-ceres.

14. Conduct a Human Capital Audit

I introduced the concept of Job Re-designing previously. Your employee's performance is what they do. Their performance is what they are truly capable of doing. The problem with measuring performance alone to gauge your people's value is that most of the time, organizations do an extremely poor job of measuring their employee's performance.

In addition, most of the budget they spend on their employees is wasted. Why? Because when organizations hire individuals to perform a job, they are in effect hiring that employee to perform a very finite set of roles and responsibilities. In order to hire the right individual to perform a pre-defined set of tasks they fail to take into consideration that individual's many other skills, background, experience that could be leveraged for additional gain. They are in effect missing out on all of the other capabilities their people bring to the organization.

Therefore, it is extremely beneficial to conduct an audit of all the collective skills your workforce possess that are NOT being leveraged. Such a formal audit is called a Human Capital Audit. As a means of assisting my clients in uncovering the skills that their employees possess that weren't being utilized, I developed a Web-based platform called a Human Capital Audit that enables organizations to identify the skills their people are NOT currently utilizing in the jobs they perform.

Here's how you can conduct a systemic, organization-wide assessment of the collective skills your people possess that are not being leveraged. You can then take a performance management planning approach to design an action plan to assist your people in incorporating ALL of their untapped talents in their day to day work.

Begin by listing each employee's roles that they currently are tasked with performing. It is their current collection of responsibilities.

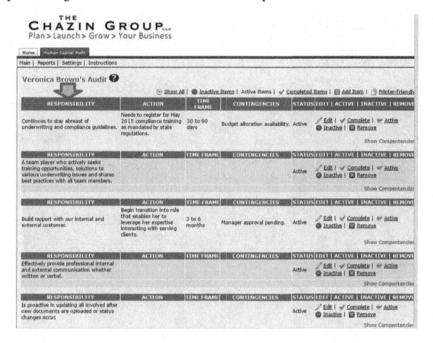

Define the Action(s) required by the employee, her Manager, and others to obtain the new skills and roles being added to her existing responsibilities.

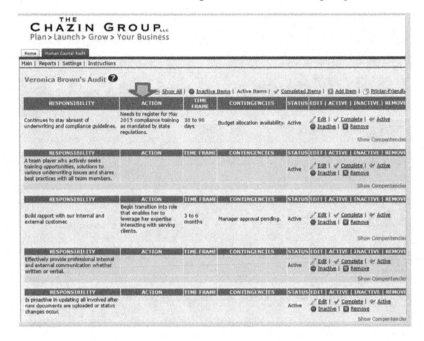

Set the Timeframe for the employee to complete the required actions associated with obtaining that new task/role/responsibility.

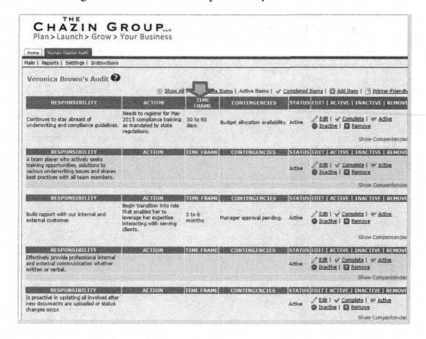

Identify and plan for any/all Contingencies, those potential barriers that may prevent the employee from acquiring that new task/role.

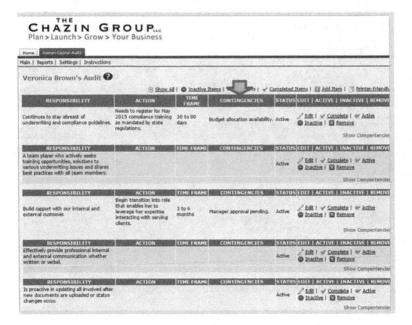

Add new roles and responsibilities for the employee as they arise and use those newly added roles as a method for maintaining an ongoing dialog with your people.

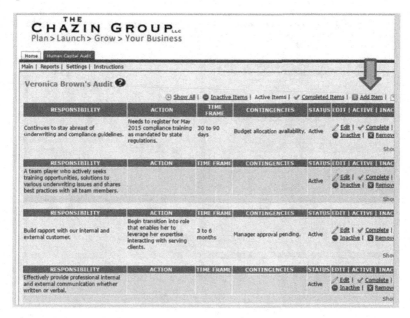

Add the new role/responsibility to the employee's Audit, the action(s) required to obtain that new task, and any contingencies that may prevent them from successfully acquiring that new role.

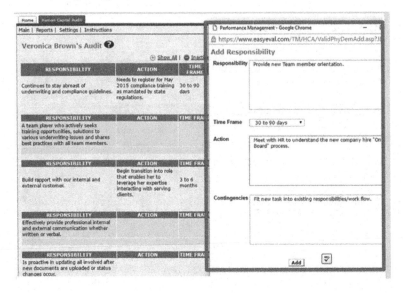

15. A New Model for Trust

Organizational trust is an extremely interesting phenomenon. In the 20th Century command-control organizational structure, employees were forced to trust without question the strategy, goals and motives of the organization. In the Employer-Employee contract, the employer held all of the power, as employees were, and still are, employed at the whim of the employer. Given the one-sided nature of the relationship, the complete control held by the Employer led and often still leads to the abuse of such power.

> **"Power tends to corrupt, and absolute power corrupts absolutely." Lord Action**

However, with the embrace of more compassionate organizations, the balance of power seems to be finally shifting. Certainly, many organizations are being led in such a manner that the Employer's power is not being abused.

In this new business climate in which organizations are behaving with more compassion, it is the perfect time for us to revisit the very idea of TRUST. In the *old* model of trust, if we trusted another person, then we felt confident with them and we tended to engage with them. If we do not trust another person, then we generally do not engage with them or not in a fully open manner. Or if we do engage, we become what is known as a "cordial hypocrite" by having interactions that are not based on trust. We're civil, but totally insincere.

There are two completely opposite types of trust that exist: "Simple and Blind."

1. Simple Trust: Is completely child-like trust. It is simple and pure and unquestioned.

2. Blind Trust: It's an aspect of being in denial. Psychologically speaking, we shut out the concepts of uncomfortable thoughts that might detract from the trust we have in another. For example, trusting a parent, guardian, or loved one when they have exhibited behaviors that call into question our faith in them. Blind trust is often bestowed on all-powerful leaders, such as cult figures.

A Common (Middle) Ground for Trust.

These two types of trust lack any middle ground. I propose that that organizations that wish to become compassionate cultures for employee success embrace MATURE trust as such a middle ground.

Mature Trust is the belief that a trusting relationship starts with an element of inherent mistrust that all individuals share towards others. Consider it a common human understanding that there is a potential for mistrust to develop in any relationship. We all start new (work) relationships with an implicit trust with our peers, co-workers, boss, vendors, etc. that is based on an agreement and understanding of our roles and responsibilities. We're in effect giving them the benefit of the doubt. The mindset is, I was hired to perform work tasks, and as part of a Team and this organization I trust that you will work with me to ensure we all are successful in completing the work we were assigned.

Trust needs to be tested, verified, and renewed over time repeatedly. It is based on our actions, rather than feelings. The reason we engage with others in organizations is we derive mutual benefit from the successful outcomes of working in teams, and feel joy when we achieve accomplishments with our peers.

What does mutual trust look like when organizations don't abuse the power they hold over employees? TD Industries is a privately held construction company in Dallas, TX that has embraced a principle known as "servant leadership" since 1970. TD Industries uses a number of best practices for its leaders to engage their teams in such a way as to ensure they don't exploit the company's workers but enable them to flourish. For example, employees evaluate supervisors, and their evaluations determine Supervisor salaries and promotion potential. [109]

---

[109] "When Power Doesn't Corrupt." The NY Times. May 27, 2017. Matthew Hutson.

16. The (Negative) Impact of Bad Work

The U.S. is the MOST Overworked Developed Nation in THE WORLD. This is not subjective bias but actual fact. According to the Center for American Progress on the topic of work and family life balance, "in 1960, only 20 percent of mothers worked. Today, 70 percent of American children live in households where all adults are employed." Regardless of which parent works and who stays home, when all adults are working (single or with a partner), that's a huge hit to the American family and free-time in the American household.

More important than whether both parents are working or how many hours parents are away from the home at work, parents who hate their jobs bring their stress and ill will home with them and children often suffer. The U.S. is the **ONLY** country in the Americas without a national paid parental leave benefit. The average is over 12 weeks of paid leave anywhere other than Europe and over 20 weeks in Europe.[110]

- The White-Collar Sweatshop by *Jill Andresky Fraser*
- The Overworked American by *Juliet Schor*
- The Working Life by *Joanne B. Ciulla*

Overworked leads to MORE Stress, Leading to:

- Fatigue
- High Blood Pressure
- Heart Disease
- Overeating
- Substance Abuse
- Lost Time With Loved Ones
- Spousal/Child Abuse

---

[110] https://20somethingfinance.com/american-hours-worked-productivity-vacation.

- Anger Management/Road Rage
- Early Death
- Suicide

Stronger Interpersonal Communication for Better Work Environments

"I'm sorry. You were right. I was wrong!"

In organizations that act with civility and respect for one another, there is a healthy communication style that permeates interpersonal relationships.

In compassionate organizations, these types of phrases are commonplace. In many other dysfunctional organizations, they're not. Which begs the question when it comes to optimal communication styles between employees, "Why are these words so hard for people to say... and mean?"

After all, this is one of the first things we learn to say as a child and yet some adults are still incapable of saying and meaning these things. For anyone who is or has been married, this may seem like a lead into a joke. You know, when a comedian says something like: "I tell you, with my wife I can't win. Even when I'm right, I'm wrong."

But quite a few situations have come up recently which is making me question whether anyone really knows how to say "I'm sorry" or "you're right, I was wrong" anymore. What is going on with these *non-apologists*?

And I think this is a really powerful thing for us to confront, because the inability to admit one is wrong seems to have a direct correlation with their ability to have meaningful, long-term and constructive relationships which in turn affects people's careers, work and their very livelihood.

An example...

A career coaching client of mine that I worked with years ago emailed me out of the blue asking for my mailing address. She said she wanted to send a thank you gift as a sign of appreciation, for my helping to coach her by offering her a very significant discounted rate in order to accommodate her circumstances.

So, I emailed it to her. Immediately thereafter, she began emailing me these bizarre, obtuse messages about how she is so misunderstood, and she deals with so many pressures in having to be true to who she is being ethical, and feels attacked.

When I emailed her back finally in effect asking: "What the heck are you talking about?" she stopped emailing me. No apology. no further explanation. Long story short, her gift came, she's still looking for full-time employment, and I have no idea what she was talking about.

Or this...

Another coaching client committed to introduce me to the head of his organization's training & development Department, in order to see if they would like to have me do training there.

I left him many follow up voice mails and emails inquiring about it, but I never heard back from him.

I finally confronted him on it. He got defensive. *I apologized* if he felt I was being unduly harsh during a one and half hour conversation we had afterwards.

During our talk, I proceeded to give him considerable guidance on how to continue thriving in his job...THAT I HELPED HIM GET. Well, he subsequently made an introduction on my behalf as he promised. But rather than simply say "I'm sorry" *he said he did not want to work together anymore*.

What I find so troubling is, this behavior seems to be EVERYWHERE. Athletes fail drug tests, cheat, abuse women. Say nothing. Police are being accused of all sorts of misconduct, from planting evidence to racially motivated violence towards civilians, to downright murder. Say nothing. Politicians... lawyers...nothing!

I like this list of five reasons why **some people struggle with apologizing, even when they KNOW they're in the wrong**:

Check out this link online: https://www.psychologytoday.com/blog/the-squeaky-wheel/201305/5-reasons-why-some-people-will-never-say-sorry/

17. Effective Communications

"In a global marketplace, it is absolutely critical
that we communicate effectively, to achieve
our organizational goals." - Me, 2012

What is the purpose of communicating? How do compassionate organizations use the three-pronged approach of communication (written, verbal, and non-verbal) to foster stronger relationships, while maintaining open lines of dialog that lead to lasting competitive advantage?

Through my years of employee training & development, executive coaching and consulting, I can declare that it is ALWAYS best to OVER-communicate. Organizations get into trouble when they fail to communicate.

A. The Written Word

We begin with the first of the three communication strategies...written communication. What is the "purpose" of writing?

We write in order to accomplish the following:

- Explain or justify the actions we have already taken.
- Convey information.
- Influence the reader to take a desired action.
- Deliver good/bad news.
- Direct the reader towards a desired action. [112]

---

[111] R. Inkster and J. M. Kilborn, *The Writing of Business*, Allyn and Bacon, 1999.
[112] http://grammar.about.com/od/ab/g/businesswritingterm.htm

"Writing is making sense of life." - Nadine Gordimer

Poor Writing Leads to Poor Organizational Results

A Net Future Institute Research study revealed that with respect to <u>online</u> communication, the issue isn't sending/receiving ENOUGH email, but the inability of the writer to GET THEIR POINT ACROSS. To wit:

- One in three US workers write poorly.
- Poorly written business communications wastes time, drains resources, and causes errors. (HR Magazine. June, 2006)
- 85% of survey respondents said poor communications wastes time, 70% cited lost productivity (HR Magazine. April, 2006)

<u>BEFORE</u> you start writing, ask yourself the following questions:

- What's the situation/problem/issue that is prompting me to write this?
- Why am I writing this document?
- Who is going to read it?
- What do your readers need to know?
- What action do you want your readers to take?

Good business writing DEMANDS you know what you are doing. Have a 60-second conversation with yourself BEFORE you begin. This will enable you to avoid the many mistakes that come from taking a "READY-FIRE-AIM" approach to your communication.

Outline *Versus* Free Writing Styles

Free writing is a prewriting technique in which a person writes continuously for a set period of time without regard to spelling, grammar, or topic. It produces raw, often unusable material, but it will help you to overcome the initial mental blocks often associated with lacking passion for the topic and any self-criticism you bring to the task.

Free writing is used to collect one's initial thoughts and ideas on a topic, often as a preliminary first step towards a more formal writing effort. (Wikipedia)

Your Communication Strategy

A communications strategy consists of five (5) variables that the writer needs to take into consideration:

- Communicator (Writer) Strategy
- Audience Strategy
- Message Strategy
- Channel Choice Strategy
- Culture Strategy

Next, you will need to define your communication objectives. What is it that you want to achieve, as a direct outcome of sending the communication?

- GENERAL: The broad overall goal for the communication. It's primary purpose.
- ACTION: A series of action outcomes – specific, measurable, time-sensitive steps required, to accomplish general objective(s.) What are the things that you want to happen as a result of sending the communication?
- COMMUNICATION: The overall physical output/format that you hope to achieve from a specific communication effort. Is it a report, an email, presentation, memo?

Two Communication Styles to Use

- **Join/Consult Approach:** In the 'join/consult' approach, you are looking to learn from the audience. You are applying an "inquiry" style. Consult is exactly what it sounds like. A collaborative approach. Join is even more collaborative. You are actively engaged in the communication effort. Think "brainstorming" as an example.
- **Tell/Sell Approach:** When you want your audience to learn from you. In 'tell' mode, you inform or explain something. In SELL, you are attempting to persuade/advocate for something through the communication.[113]

---

[113] Tannenbaum & Schmidt. Study of Leadership.

Establish subject matter expertise in your field. It is important to know what your audience's perception of your initial credibility is. What do they think of you?

- Factors that determine credibility:
  - Rank
  - Goodwill
  - Expertise
  - Image
  - Common ground

Your Audience Strategy consists of:

- Who are they?
- What do they know and expect?
- What do they feel?
- What will persuade them?

Your Message Strategy includes:

- Key points
- Key questions
- Steps in a process
- Alternatives to compare

The 4-Step Communication Process

STEP 1: You establish your overall communication strategy, beginning with your audience and desired outcomes.

STEP 2: Determine whether you want/need to write your communication, or deliver it verbally. The size and geographic location of the audience, the need to be "in-front" of the audience to read their reactions, and the sense of urgency/timeliness in conducting will determine your method selected.

STEP 3: IF you decide to deliver your communication in written format, then break down your activities into the following FIVE (5) steps:

- Research your topic, subject matter, industry trends, available data to support your position, etc.

- Organize your thoughts into a cohesive format.
- Focus the information on the specific goal(s) you have.
- Draft a first working template, then perfect through the editorial process.
- The Editorial process entails a number of re-writes, which may include having someone else/others review and provide feedback. May help to have an advocate, someone whose position/expertise/ experience you trust or perhaps someone that is diametrically opposed to your position involved in the editorial review process.

STEP 4: Factor in any/all feedback you received, rethink your strategy, re-organize your format/content, and then make any/all necessary final changes.

Organizational Communication for Employee Benefit

Organizations have a significant responsibility to maintain an open and ongoing line of communication with their employees, especially in larger "pyramid" shaped organizations with many layers of employee reporting structure from bottom front-line staff up to the "C" suite.

The different types of communication tools used by the organization are only limited by that organization's desire to communicate and its collective creativity. Communication tools can and should include:

- E-newsletters;
- The organization's website;
- Employee Intranet site;
- Email;
- Manager-direct report meetings;
- Social media platforms and YouTube;
- Manager-Team meetings;
- Leader-Department/Business Unit;
- Onsite HQ Town Halls with remote office connections;
- Off-site retreats

Meetings can be held weekly, bi-weekly, monthly, quarterly, semi-annually, and annually.

Develop Your Organization's Town Hall Program

Program Goals

Create a program for senior management to communicate the company's performance to all of your employees, the media, business partners, consultants, etc. in an informal fashion on a regular basis (quarterly to coincide with quarterly updates is the most common scheduling for such a program.)

All offices and locations must participant in-person or at the very least via videoconference. Tape the session so that employees that are unable to attend in-person can view the program afterwards, at their convenience.

Cross-Functional Participation Required

Select the appropriate candidates to represent a cross-functional team assigned to manage all logistical consideration surrounding implementing and maintaining such a program. The leadership driving such a program typically comes from Marketing or the Human Resources Departments.

Senior Management Presentations

The members of the executive team should present on the quarterly performance of the Company as a whole, as well as such key areas as sales, marketing, finance, operations, Research 7 Product Development.

Media Coverage

Invite the media to attend the event in order to generate press coverage. Distribute the presentations in advance to all employees.

Encourage Honest Q&A Dialog

Provide index cards for each location facilitator to distribute to attendees. Have the facilitator collect them and read the questions to the Senior Management Team. Make it possible for employees that didn't get to ask questions during the event to submit them later. Distribute the answers to the entire company by email, mail.

Technical/Logistical Arrangements

Arrange a videoconference session to show the videotape and the presentations. Make it a point to have a special acknowledgement for people/teams that completed a special project, or accomplished something special.

Town Hall Meeting Program Brief

Program Details:

Project Name:	**[Your Organization] Town Hall Program**
Project Owner:	Your Name
Start Date:	Month day, Year
Complete-By Date:	Month day, Year
Business Units That Support the Program (If applicable):	
Business Sponsor (If applicable):	Senior Management

Document Distribution:

Primary Contacts	Business Function
Name	Senior Management
Name	Finance
Name	Human Resources
Name	Sales & Marketing

Metrics to Determine Success:

- Establish revenue objectives if applicable.
- Survey attendees for message retention immediately after Town Hall is completed.

Themes/Messaging:

Our people are our inspiration.

Budget:

Item	Cost
Pre-fund the program for development, competitive information gathering, training, marketing, and other functions tied to launching and maintaining such a program.	$x,000
Reward contributors whose ideas have merit but cannot be pursued for various reasons.	$x,000
Reward contributors whose ideas are deemed worthy of implementation.	$x,000
Total:	**$x,000**

Production Schedule:

Action	Start Date	End Date	Owner	Status
Senior Management needs to meet to discuss program parameters. Conduct during Strategic Planning process meeting. Identify likely participants for the cross-functional Project Team.	x/x/2017	x/x/2017	To be determined	Open
Share program details with the Company.	x/x/2017	x/x/2017	To be determined	Open
First meeting of cross-functional Project Management Team.	x/x/2017	x/x/2017	To be determined	Open
Develop idea submission form.	x/x/2013	x/x/2013	To be determined	Open

Promotional Campaign:

Initiative	Owner	Start Date	End Date	Status
Distribute internal email.	TBD	x/x/2017	x/x/2017	Open
Promote program via company newsletter.	TBD	x/x/2017	x/x/2017	Open
Discuss during Town Hall meeting.	TBD	x/x/2017	x/x/2017	Open

Contingencies Impacting Completion:

- Receive approval from Senior Management.
- Enlist participants of the Cross-Functional Team.
- Budget for pre-funding the program.

B. The Spoken Word

<u>The Power of Effective Public Speaking.</u>

A while back, I attended a networking event that was held at a local community bank. One of the bank representatives stood up to give a talk about the banks' exceptional track record in providing their small business banking customers with loans.

He had a golden opportunity, spoke for only few minutes...*and he proceeded to completely lose the crowd!*

He appeared like a nice enough fellow, was extremely knowledgeable, yet he understood **NOTHING** about the art of speaking as a means of "storytelling."

All I could think of as he spoke was: *"Please stop...please stop...PLEASE STOP!"* followed by: **"Watching paint dry would be more exciting than listening to him!"**

Clearly, I wasn't alone. Glancing around the room, I spotted many folks attempting (with varying degrees of success) to discreetly check their emails on their phones. When presented with a unique opportunity to "pitch" his services to a captive and willing audience of existing customers, this individual (and the bank that hosted the event) lost the crowd.

He droned on and on, using a monotone and uninspiring voice while rocking gently back and forth. He was doing his darnedest to put us all asleep. **It felt like he was trying to hypnotize us.** All because he lacked BASIC public speaking skills.

I've seen this type of public speaking ineptitude too many times to count. So, following is my **13-STEP public speaking diva action plan** that I use to teach public speaking perfection to my clients. Follow these and you'll become a public-speaking diva in NO time.

Some basic guidelines to start things off…

- Prepare what you're going to say.
- Start with the opening. (Say what you're going to say)
- Provide a preview of your main points.
- Clearly separate your main points.
- ENGAGE…ENGAGE…ENGAGE (say it)
- Be **COMPELLING!**
- The CLOSE! Tell them what you said.

The Opening of your talk REALLY matters.

- You have 3-5 seconds to hook the audience in, or face the threat of losing their attention.
- Tell them WHY you're speaking to them (What are you going to say.)
- Show them the WIIFM – 'what's in it for me?'
- Build your credibility as the subject matter expert.
- Use humor with caution.

1. Your Talk Is Not About YOU.

Understand that the situation (your presentation) isn't about YOU. **Always focus on the needs of your audience, and the best way for you to serve them.**

In the example that I provided in my intro, I was referring to an all too common pattern of behavior that people exhibit when they speak. It's called: "**selfish communication**." Here are a few warning signs that you are guilty of this when you present:

- You approach the audience from a **ME** perspective.
- You **DON'T** add value.
- You **ASSUME** they care about what you have to say.
- You don't tailor the message to the audience.

2. Let Your Passion Show

There is no substitute for authentic passion at the podium. When you believe in your message and have energy around your topic, it will translate to your audience. Above all else, *be yourself* up there!

> *"There are three things to aim at in public speaking: first, to get into your subject, then to get your subject into yourself, and lastly, to get your subject into the heart of your audience."*
> *- Alexander Gregg*

3. Prepare and Practice.

If you're giving a high-stakes presentation like presenting to a Board or group of investors, you CAN'T leave ANYTHING to chance. Have your presentation prepared well in advance, so you have lots of time to practice. There truly is no substitute for preparation.

"**Winging it**" is a risky strategy that few people can pull off. You need a well thought out roadmap (OUTLINE) of what you're going to say, and *rehearse often*. Like the answer to the famous saying: "How do you get to Carnegie hall, practice, practice, practice," there is tremendous value in perfecting every aspect of your presentation. This includes the content of your presentation, hand gestures and non-verbal cues, voice inflexion…everything.

4. Connect with Your Audience.

It will help you tremendously to get to know the audience you are presenting to. As you craft your speech keep asking yourself: "**So what…who cares?**"

This simple yet powerful technique is amazing for helping you focus on the needs, wants, and desires of your audience.

One mistake speakers often make is trying to *prove we're smart*. Remember, you're at the podium for a reason. Your credentials speak for themselves. When we stand in front of an audience, there is already a gap — you're the expert, they're not.

By trying to impress your audience with your intellect, you create more distance and could come across as arrogant. Your job as presenters is to close the gap, not widen it. Be humorous and **real** so you're approachable. The more connected the audience feels to you, the more they'll pay attention to what you have to say.

5. Stick to Your Strengths.

As a general rule, you should always be talking about things you are really good at and are passionate about.

6. Focus on Your Goal(s).

Before you start working on your script or presentation, get clear on its purpose. What are you trying to accomplish? What impact do you want to have on your audience? Are you looking to inform? Inspire? Persuade? Knowing your ultimate purpose and desired outcome will help you stay focused through the preparation process.

7. Simplify Your Message.

You are where you are because of the depth and breadth of your expertise. Your natural inclination will be to impart lots of that knowledge onto your audience. **Resist that urge!**

Otherwise, you'll bore and overwhelm your listeners with details they'll never retain. Focus on conveying a few powerful ideas that they'll remember. Think of yourself as a **Master Distiller of Information** – boil it down to its most basic messaging.

> ## "No one ever complains about a speech being too short!" - Ira Hayes

8. Avoid Death by PowerPoint.

Death by PowerPoint persists. You know those speakers. You've suffered through their talks MANY times. If you have to use a presentation software consider using alternatives to PowerPoint, such as Prezi or Slide Rocket.

Hat tip to one of my readers **Carl E. Reid** for mentioning Guy Kawasaki's **"10/20/30 Rule of PowerPoint."** Use 10 slides for a 20-minute talk using 30-point font.

If you MUST use PowerPoint, then follow these guidelines to minimize the effect of audience members tuning out:

- Use headlines and sub-headlines liberally.
- Choose your colors wisely based on the emotional effect colors have.
- Match your choice of text with background color for optimal visual effect.
- Maintain consistent "LOOK" BUT...mix up your slides to maintain interest.
- Incorporate a wide range of graphics including: charts, pie charts, graphs to depict your message in as visually compelling way as you can.
- Cite your sources at the bottom of the applicable slides.
- Check for errors - have someone you trust proof-read.
- Design slides to tell a story of WHY & HOW!
- Spacing matters. Use LOTS of white space. Emulate the Apple website design approach.
- Acclimate yourself to the equipment and the venue beforehand.

9. Make It Personal with Stories.

Storytelling puts an audience at ease, humanizes you as a speaker, and makes your messages more memorable. It is the most powerful tool in a speaker's toolkit. To find your stories, you simply have to mine your own life experiences and pull out the gems.

Audiences will remember your stories more easily than facts and figures, and they're more likely to enjoy your presentation. Another benefit is

that personal stories are easier for *you* to remember when you're at the podium.

10. Watch Yourself.

Few tools are as instructive as video playback. People can tell you that you wander the stage, over-gesture, slouch, have an incessantly grim facial expression or use a repetitive speech pattern, but once you see it on tape, it will be much easier for you to grasp and change. If you prefer to rehearse in private, use your iPad or hand-held device's video feature. Stand in front of it and let it roll!

11. Avoid Sameness.

It is said that *sameness is the enemy of speaking*. If you follow the same cadence, vocal rhythm, pitch, tone and gesture patterns throughout your presentation, your audience *will* tune you out.

Think about what puts a baby to sleep. Or a robot! You need to mix things up; keep enough variety in your delivery so it holds the audience's interest.

12. Work that Body…Work That Body!

90+% of communication is nonverbal. Your audience will read your facial expressions, the tone of your voice, the way you use your hands, how you stand and move. A warm, easy smile and calm body immediately tell the audience that you're comfortable and confident. And when the speaker is comfortable, the audience is, too.

Be aware of your body language. Watch the TED talk by Amy Cuddy on the power of body language.

13. Check Out the Venue Beforehand.

If possible, visit the location where you will be giving your talk in advance. Familiarity with the venue helps to reduce the stress associated with giving a presentation.

There you have it. A tried & true 13-step blueprint for public speaking success! What do you think? Let me know if you'd like to discuss ways I can help you get your public speaking diva on.

Craft a Compelling Elevator Pitch

The elevator pitch is your presentation of who you are, what you do, and who you do it for.

Got its name because you should be able to deliver that message in the 30 seconds or so it takes to ride an elevator to the top floor with a complete stranger and sell them on YOU. The sad truth is, in our ADD society we no longer have those precious 30 seconds to make an impression at business networking events with strangers.

There is a guideline to networking when it comes to the elevator pitch. It is called the "**5-2-1 rule.**"

You have five seconds to say something so profound that they ask you wow what does that mean take 2 minutes explaining and be so impactful that you get the one-hour meeting scheduled after the networking event. Something like: "I'm Ethan Chazin, I transform people's lives" works like a charm.

You should be able to reel off your elevator pitch at any time, from a job interview to a cocktail party conversation or a networking event with someone who might be able to help you or in need of what you do.

Sounds simple, right? But condensing your entire life's accomplishments into a 30-second statement that packs a punch can be overwhelming. Following is my 9-step process that can be used to convert even the most boring pitches into a world-class elevator presentation.

1. Clarify your target.

When you begin putting your elevator pitch together, nail down the best way to describe what you can offer based on the audience. You probably will have several prepared for any situation.

2. Put it on paper.

Write down everything you'd want a stranger to know about you, then grab a red pen and mercilessly delete everything that's not critical to your pitch. Keep editing until you've got the speech down to a few key bullet points or sentences. Your goal is to interest the listener in learning more, not to tell your whole life story. Remove extraneous details that detract from your core message.

3. Format it.

A good pitch should answer three questions: Who are you? What do you do? What are you looking for?

4. Tailor the pitch to *them*, not *you*.

It's important to remember that the people listening to your speech will have their antennas tuned to WIFM (What's in It for Me?) So be sure to focus your message on *their* needs.

5. Eliminate industry jargon.

You need to make your pitch easy for anyone to understand, so avoid using acronyms and tech-speak that the average person might not understand. The last thing you want to do is make your listener feel stupid or uninformed.

6. Read your pitch out loud.

Reading it aloud then tinkering with the words will help you sound more authentic.

7. Practice then solicit feedback.

Rehearse your pitch in front of a mirror or use the recording capabilities of your computer, so you can see and hear how you sound. This might feel awkward at first, but the more you practice, the smoother your delivery will be.

Keep tweaking your pitch until it no longer sounds rehearsed. When your presentation is polished to your satisfaction, try it out on a few friends and ask them what they thought your key points were. If their response doesn't square with your objective, the speech still needs work.

8. Prepare a few variations.

You might want to say things slightly differently to different audiences. Also, sometimes you'll just have 15 seconds for a pitch (kind of a short elevator ride), other times you may have a minute or two. Focus on mastering a few talking points then work up ways to customize your speech for particular situations. Word count feature on your computer to create shorter and longer pitches; a good rule of thumb is that you can say about 150 words in one minute.

9. Nail it with confidence.

The best-worded elevator pitch in the world will fall flat unless it's conveyed well. When you give the speech, look the person in the eye, smile and deliver your message with a confident, upbeat delivery.

In Closing.

When it comes to public speaking, nothing beats preparation. Get as much practice as you can, speak from your heart on topics you know and love, and make a connection with the audience. Part of establishing powerful relationships when you meet someone for the first time is to craft an engaging and compelling elevator pitch.

How to Conduct Effective Meetings.

- We expect people to engage/ participate but get annoyed when they talk TOO MUCH.

- We want people to be comprehensive, thoughtful and innovative, yet FAST and efficient.
- We expect people to provide their best ideas but not get defensive when we modify or reject them.
- We hold people to high standards and expect them not to get caught in "GROUPTHINK" but resent when they don't follow along with the group.
- People have their own opinions, objectives and agendas.
- There is always a POLITICAL environment that presents barriers.
- Members differ in their cultural, personality, experience, values, and belief systems.

Bad business communication leads to:

- Decreased productivity.
- Low employee morale.
- Mistakes.
- Damaged relationships with: clients, vendors, partners, suppliers, share-holders, the media.
- Unclear employee roles.
- Wasted resources.

C. Body Language

Nonverbal communication is …the process of communication through sending and receiving wordless (mostly visual) messages between people. Messages can be communicated through gestures and touch, by body language or posture, by facial expression and eye contact. Nonverbal messages could also be communicated through material exponential; meaning, objects or artifacts (such as clothing, hairstyles or architecture). Speech contains nonverbal elements known as paralanguage, including voice quality, rate, pitch, volume, and speaking style, as well prosodic features such as rhythm, intonation, and stress.

Body language can be the most powerful of the three communication styles, especially when mastered. Start by embracing the sensitivity of everything we discussed in Emotional Intelligence, couple that empathy, trust and caring with the power of public speaking and giving effective presentations, and you are ready to take on the world.

For a primer, I strongly suggest you watch **Amy Cuddy's** TED talk entitled: "Your body language shapes who you are."[114]

She makes the case that we should always be tapped into our body posture and how it is making us feel at that moment. Sounds an awful LOT like emotional awareness, right?

Power Posing

She shows how "power posing" -- standing in a posture of confidence, even when we don't feel confident -- can affect testosterone and cortisol levels in the brain, and might even have an impact on our chances for success and how our lives unfold.

Examples

I'm focused on you, fully engaged, paying complete attention, and VERY favorably disposed to what you have to say.

I'm concentrating and fully engaged. Can't you tell from my furrowed b row and hand resting at the side of my head?

---

[114] https://www.youtube.com/watch?v=Ks-_Mh1QhMc.

Body Language Varies by Culture

It is critically important that anyone that works with people from different cultures understand how body postures differ by region. Some examples:

- In India, Africa, and the Middle East, people always use their right hand for greeting, touching, and eating. They consider the left hand unclean, so you should never use it for anything publicly.
- Several cultures consider crossing your legs to be rude. For example, in the Middle East and South Africa, crossed legs often show the sole of the foot, a sign of an ill wish or a bad omen. In Japan, it's considered rude to cross your legs in the presence of someone older or more respected than you.
- Certain gestures considered acceptable in one country can be highly offensive in another. For example, a "thumbs up" gesture is seen as a sign of satisfaction in the West, but is highly offensive in some Middle Eastern countries.
- In the United States, a handshake demonstrates that negotiations are finished, and that everyone is leaving on good terms. In the Middle East, a handshake is a sign that serious negotiations are now beginning.
- In many cultures, pointing is impolite, so it's usually best to avoid it entirely. If you must gesture toward something, use your entire hand.[115]

Hofstede's Six Dimensions of Culture

Psychologist Dr. Geert Hofstede published his cultural dimensions model at the end of the 1970s, based on a decade of research. Since then, it's become an internationally recognized standard for understanding cultural differences. Hofstede studied people who worked for IBM in more than 50 countries. Initially, he identified four dimensions that could distinguish one culture

---

[115] www.mindtools.com/pages/article/cross-cultural-mistakes.htm. "Avoiding cross-cultural faux pas".

from another. Later, he added fifth and sixth dimensions, in cooperation with Drs. Michael H. Bond and Michael Minkov. [116] These are:

1. Power Distance Index (high versus low).
2. Individualism Versus Collectivism.
3. Masculinity Versus Femininity.
4. Uncertainty Avoidance Index (high versus low).
5. Pragmatic Versus Normative.
6. Indulgence Versus Restraint.

In the TED talk, "How to kill your body language Frankenstein and inspire the villagers", Scott Rouse says that 87% of everything we "think" that we know is wrong, meaning our assumptions are not supported by research. This is where we can (and often do) get into trouble when we rely on what we think we know about reading the physical cues others are sending us. Our assumptions lead us to misunderstandings.

"Body Language, the power is in the palm of your hands" TED talk by **Allan Pease**. So much non-verbal communication goes into the deceptively complicated act of the handshake. [117]

Non-verbal cues:

- *Mirroring* technique is when you literally "match" the posture and positioning of the person in front of you. Research shows that when you do this, you put the other person at ease.
- Lean in to express interest.
- Avoid eye-rolling, turning your back, yawning, and talking over others.
- Arm-crossing is a universal danger posture. It entails crossing arms over your torso which is a defensive position to literally protect your vital organs. It sends a number of negative messages from a lack of trust, feeling threatened, and being turned off by someone.

---

[116] www.mindtools.com/pages/article/newLDR_66.htm. "Hofstede's cultural dimensions."

[117] www.youtube.com/watch?v=ZZZ7k8cMA-4. Macquarie University. Nov. 17, 2013

18. Lead, Don't Manage

Why Leadership is Critical to Your Organization's Success.

The DEFINITION of True Leadership...

Let's start with the question that lies at the heart of any discussion on leadership...

"What makes a leader?"

It is extremely difficult to provide an adequate answer, because the word has such drastically different and heart-felt meanings depending on who you ask. Descriptions abound from noted figures across all areas including the political domain, heads of state, leaders of business and industry...everyone seems to have a different opinion as to what makes a GREAT leader.

Great leadership quotes to inspire:

Margaret Meade alluded to the power of change that a small group of passionate people can achieve when she said: "**Never doubt that a small group of committed individuals can change the world. Indeed, it's the only thing that ever has.**"

Napoleon Bonaparte was famous for saying: "**A leader is a dealer in hope.**" In his estimation, leadership could be summed up as providing encouragement to others that you will lead them to the bright future of tomorrow. When you give people HOPE, you have provided them with a very powerful gift that will see you through turbulent times.

Elaine Agather, CEO of Chase Manhattan bank commented that: "**The leadership instinct you are born with is the backbone. You develop the funny bone and the wishbone that go with it.**" Leadership to her entails having the strength to pursue your goals even through the most challenging of times, while keeping a sense of humor and the ability to hold out hope for the best outcomes.

It was **St. Augustine** who said: "**Do you wish to rise? Begin by descending. You plan a tower that will pierce the clouds? Lay first the foundation of humility.**" Such a definition of leadership touches on the very essence of what a true leader can become.

When you analyze the great contributions of others and try to explain the meaning of great leadership, you come away with the feeling that to be a truly great leader, you MUST inspire others to accomplish great deeds by exhibiting yourself the kind of qualities that you would expect from others.

It means consistently striving to achieve greatness by taking risks. The most effective leaders share a common attribute that they have had a "positive" impact on the lives of the people that they came into contact with. It entails nothing less ambitious than touching other people's lives.

Applying Leadership to Business

What it will take for you to succeed in business? What traits can be identified as most critical for you to succeed? Success begins with an inherent desire to follow an **ethical code of behavior,** or doing what you know is right. Entrepreneurs and small business owners are in a unique position, in that the organizations they are creating can be strongly influenced by their own personal moral compass. When you just start out as a new business owner, your value system becomes the culture of the organization you are creating.

There have been MANY examples that serve to warn us what happens when business leaders set aside morality in the pursuit of profit. What can be learned about the value of ethics in defining leaders when we look at the behavior and impact that people like Bernie Madoff and the executives at companies like Enron, Worldcom, Arthur Andersen, Tyco, Global Crossing, Countrywide, Goldman Sachs, Adelphia have had?

These "leaders" stole hundreds of millions of dollars from their businesses, which drove their companies into bankruptcy and harmed their employees and investors. Other organizations like AIG, Bear Stearns, Lehman Brothers, Merrill Lynch, Fannie Mae, Freddie Mac, were woefully mismanaged due to a pronounced lack of leadership.

For Starters, Believe in Yourself.

You have to have an absolute **belief in your abilities** which will come in time from achieving success in leading others. Your **vision** consists in seeing future outcomes before others can. You must gain experience working in and driving Teams comprised of people from different backgrounds who have different values, beliefs, and personalities towards a common set of goals. Start by taking advantage of any and all opportunities to lead Teams either in work settings, volunteer work, PTAs, Girl/Boy Scout clubs, wherever the opportunities arise.

Strive to achieve excellence in everything you do. And with everything you do in business as in life, be passionate. **Life is too short to settle on an uninspired existence.** Another universal quality shared by all great leaders is a driving concern for the well-being of the others they have led.

Leadership and Management Are NOT the Same.

Management is detrimental; **leadership is critical** to organizational success.

HERE'S WHY...

MANAGEMENT	LEADERSHIP
• "Management" (from Old French ménagement "the art of **conducting, directing"**, • From Latin manu agere "to **lead by the hand**") characterizes the process of leading and directing all or part of an organization, often a business, through the deployment and manipulation of resources (human, financial, material, intellectual or intangible.)	• Possess a VISION. • A person who **builds consensus, guides, or inspires** others. • Refers to the position or office of an **authority figure**. • The ability to **get people to follow** willingly. • About **behavior** first, **skills** second. • Creates "buy in".

Develop Great Decision-Making Skills.

- Don't make decisions that aren't yours to make.
- Choose from alternatives, not "Right & Wrong."

Leaders understand that a successful decision-making process includes many different potential options and not merely a right or wrong choice.

- Avoid rushed decisions. A rush to judgment or quick decision-making means losing out on the benefit of weighing options or assessing long-term implications of your decision. While there is a detrimental aspect of waiting too long to make a decision "paralysis of analysis" it is also a recipe for disaster to make decisions in the "heat of the moment."

- Do your decision-making on paper: It often helps to weigh the PROs and CONs of a decision by outlining on paper all of the ramifications and potential impacts (positive and negative) so make a list and spend time developing all the options before making a decision.

Becoming a Leader Means:

- **Check Yourself…Who Are You?**

Make people want to follow you. A quality of all great leaders is an ability to make others believe you are the right person to guide them. You do that by valuing them, soliciting their ideas and sharing decision-making, encourage them to achieve great results, and always portray an aura of confidence and positivity.

- **Possess Self Knowledge**

Successful leaders are universally outstanding at self-assessment. Understand your own personal strengths and weaknesses and strive to develop your strengths while overcoming your challenges through lifelong learning, continuing professional development, pursue accreditations and certifications when needed. Seek out opinions of others you trust in your personal and professional networks about YOU. It is critical for success as a leader to understand what others think of you. Ask 5 or so people whose opinion you trust what adjectives they would use to describe you. This is an exercise in assessing the personal brand that you have created and will help you adjust your brand for effective leadership.

- **Become a Role Model**

Make your words your actions: effective leaders understand that it is NEVER acceptable to use the phrase: "**Do as I say, not as I do**." People will trust you and gravitate towards you when you exemplify the highest standards and qualities that others aspire to.

- **Be a leader in your OWN image**: While it is desirable to emulate the most attractive qualities of others, you have to become a leader in your own image.
- **Hire well**: As a business owner, you will have the opportunity to hire employees. Hire the top talent. If there is an individual whose background, skills, experience, education, training, qualities, and personality are exemplary then find a place for them in your organization, whether or not they have prior experience in the role you envision. The best leaders as business owners have a gift for finding places in their organization for rising stars.
- **Speak well**: There is no way around this. Effective leaders are all GREAT Communications. You must possess the requisite communication skills in public speaking, writing, and your non-verbal communications. If you fall short, take a public speaking course (such as toastmasters) and/or professional writing for success courses.
- **Fire FAST**: the worst thing you can do as a business owner is to retain the unmotivated, inadequate and/or negative employees in your organization. They are a cancer. If you have them, then you need to get rid of them QUICKLY!
- **Develop "learning agility"**: the best leaders are all adapt at pursuing lifelong learning. You have to practice ninja-style learning agility. You may not have to be an expert in any one area but you do have to possess general skills and knowledge expertise across a VERY wide area. You may not be a "10" in any one skill, but you must be an "8" in everything.

- **Decisiveness over inclusivity**: effective leaders all share a common bond – that being their ability to reach a decision and act on that decision – not linger through indecision. Solicit feedback, ideas, and information from those around you but all great leaders take ultimate responsibility for making a decision and they make them decisively and with authority.

- **Know just enough technology**: You may not need to know every area of a technology but you need to be a generalist in most areas.

- **Manage your time:** All great leaders understand that it is impossible to be on top of all required actions at all times. Great leaders have 200-300 things they "need to get to" but are adept at prioritizing the most critical SEVERITY 1 priorities, then they move on to #2 priorities and lastly third tier prioritized items, time permitting. The only time we are ever truly managing our own time is when we are dead. Otherwise, it's a constant juggling act.

- **Work long hours**: Business owners sweat and bleed their business. There is a requirement to put in the hours. We are NOT talking about work for work sake or "busy" work but to be on top of all the myriad responsibilities requires you to put in the hours. For those who work for others, a guideline should be that you arrive at work before your boss and stay there after she/he has left for the day.

- **Create a positive environment**: Effective leaders all create work environment that set their organization apart as a place that others aspire to work at. Examples of organizations that have created a fantastic reputation for being a great place to work are: Disney, Southwest Airlines, Trader Joe's, Google, Microsoft, etc.

  Creating a world-class work environment means being PRO employee. You can accomplish this by creating employee reward and recognition programs, soliciting ideas constantly from your people and implementing their great ideas, constantly communicating with your people, celebrating victories.

  Challenge your people to apply all of their passion, creativity, and skills in their daily jobs. Reward risk-taking and recognize failures when people attempt to achieve great results. Creating a positive environment means forging a culture where you embrace change, demand greatness, and reward risk-taking.

When you build a positive environment, your culture becomes a MAJOR competitive advantage. It enables your organization to recruit (and retain) top talent, build a brand through positive PR, and your organization will even benefit by achieving a high customer care reputation.

People Are following You. Now What?

- **Serve people's needs**: Great leaders always put the needs of others first before their own. This creates trust and commands respect, in a way that makes others want to follow you. When people know that you have their best interests at heart they are going to follow you through the most difficult of times.
- **Listen hard**: Listening not a PASSIVE activity but most managers treat it that way. Truly engaged, caring people LISTEN. They are paying 100% attention, not getting distracted by emails, phone calls, or the many other daily interruptions that can prevent exceptional listening. Ask probing questions, ensure that you clarify what people are telling you to ensure you understand them, and repeat what you think you heard.
- **Keep earning the trust of others**: One you have earned someone's trust you have to work constantly to ensure you maintain it. Trust is extremely hard to regain once you have lost it. This means always being sincere, telling the truth (even when it hurts) admitting your own mistakes. A guideline for establishing and maintaining the trust of others over time is to always give credit and take the blame.
- **Pursue (EMBRACE) change**: It may be a cliché but the one true constant in today's 21st century environment is…**change is constant**. Those who lead most effectively are not afraid of change. They embrace it willingly. Change presents opportunities, status quo means standing still and that is a recipe for getting run over.
- **Share leadership**: Managers attempt (and often fail) to control and consolidate power. Leaders defer and share. They encourage their people to take ownership of their work. Great leaders reward those who take initiative. Create a workplace that encourages people to use all of their skills (you must know each person that

works for you well enough to know all of their greatest strengths, i.e. core competencies), and you must demand excellence from yourself and others.

- **Learn, practice and teach creative problem-solving strategies:** Learn, practice and teach multiple creative problem-solving techniques such as: brainstorming, brain-writing, star-bursting, the Disney creative model, provocative thinking, reframing matrices, etc.

- **Build diverse teams:** Business owners, Department leaders, and entrepreneurs are in a unique position in that they have the opportunity to build teams from the ground up by having hiring authority. The best leaders build teams that are diverse from a background, learning/education, culture, ethical, and geographic perspective. The attribute of effective team-building for leaders is always becoming more critical as we move to a more globally inter-connected society. Do not encourage "GROUP think."

You don't want people who willingly (blindly) follow the herd, and agree just to "go along." Your challenge as a great leader is to find, hire and embrace "contrarians" who will keep you and your Team honest. You want people who always ask "WHY" and "WHAT IF...?"

Despite popular belief, CONFLICT is a good think when it forces divergent ideas, strategies, and options be considered. Great organizations embrace the challenge of effectively integrating a diverse set of solutions, in order to take advantage of as many opportunities as possible.

The 11 Styles of Leadership/Management.

1. Autocratic Leadership.

The **Autocratic Leadership Style** was first described by Lewin, Lippitt, and White in 1938 as part of their work on styles of leadership. The style is sometimes referred to as the directive leadership style, and the characteristics of an autocratic style of leadership include:

- Work methods that are dictated by the autocratic leader

- Limited employee participation in most aspects of work
- Unilateral decision making by the leader

This type of leader throws their opinions and ideas at their subordinates, doesn't nurture their people, and places demands on employees. This leader tells their people what they want, and expect their commands to be followed without deviation.

Authoritarian leaders, also known as autocratic leaders, provide clear expectations for what needs to be done, when it should be done, and how it should be done. There is also a clear division between the leader and the followers. Authoritarian leaders make decisions independently with little or no input from the rest of the group.[118]

Researchers found that decision-making was less creative under authoritarian leadership. Lewin also found that it is more difficult to move from an authoritarian style to a democratic style than vice versa. Abuse of this style is usually viewed as controlling, bossy, and dictatorial.

Authoritarian leadership is best applied to situations where there is little time for group decision-making or where the leader is the most knowledgeable member of the group.

2. Bureaucratic Leadership.

The **Bureaucratic Leadership Style** was one of three leadership styles described by Max Weber (1947) along with charismatic leadership and traditional leadership styles. The bureaucratic leadership style is based on following normative rules and adhering to lines of authority. The characteristics of the bureaucratic style include:

- Leaders impose strict and systematic discipline on the followers and demand business-like conduct in the workplace;
- Leaders are empowered via the office they hold - position power;

---

[118] http://psychology.about.com/od/leadership/f/autocratic-leadership.htm

- Followers are promoted based on their ability to conform to the rules of the office; and
- Follower should obey leaders because authority is bestowed upon the leader as part of their position in the company.

This style of leadership follows a close set of standards. Everything is done in an exact, specific way to ensure safety and/or accuracy. You will often find this leadership role in a situation where the work environment is dangerous and specific sets of procedures are necessary to ensure safety.

Bureaucratic leadership skills are best utilized in jobs such as construction work, chemistry-related jobs that involve working with hazardous material, or jobs that involve working with large amounts of money.

The Benefits of Bureaucratic Leadership

A natural bureaucratic leader will tend to create detailed instructions for other members of a group.

3. Charismatic Leadership.

The charismatic leadership style is based on a form of heroism or extreme of character - almost of divine origin. The characteristics of the charismatic style include:

- Leaders are viewed as having supernatural powers and abilities, the leader is viewed as a hero by followers;
- Leaders are followed because of personal trust and the charisma the leader exhibits;
- Followers are promoted based on personal charisma they exhibit; and
- There are no formal offices of authority, power is gained through social skills.

A charismatic leader who is building a group, whether it is a political party, a cult or a business team, will often focus strongly on making the group very clear and distinct, separating it from other groups. They will then build the image of the group, in particular in the minds of their followers, as being far superior to all others.

The charismatic leader will typically attach themselves firmly to the identity of the group, such that to join the group is to become one with the leader. In doing so, they create an unchallengeable position for themselves.

Charismatic Leaders pay a great deal of attention in scanning and reading their environment, and are good at picking up the moods and concerns of both individuals and larger audiences. They then will hone their actions and words to suit the situation.

Deliberate charisma is played out in a theatrical sense, where the leader is 'playing to the house' to create a desired effect. They also make effective use of storytelling, including the use of symbolism and metaphor. Many politicians use a charismatic style, as they need to gather a large number of followers.

A charismatic leadership style can appear similar to a transformational leadership style, in that the leader injects huge doses of enthusiasm into his or her team, and is very energetic in driving others forward. However, a charismatic leader tends to believe more in him- or herself than in their team.

This can create a risk that a project, or even an entire organization, might collapse if the leader were to leave: In the eyes of their followers, success is tied up with the presence of the charismatic leader. As such, charismatic leadership carries great responsibility, and needs long-term commitment from the leader.

4. Democratic/Participative Leadership.

A Participative Leader, rather than taking autocratic decisions, seeks to involve other people in the process, possibly including subordinates, peers, superiors and other stakeholders. Often, however, as it is within the managers' whim to give or deny control to his or her subordinates, most participative activity is within the immediate team. The question of how much influence others are given thus may vary on the manager's preferences and beliefs, and a whole spectrum of participation is possible.

Although a democratic leader will make the final decision, he or she invites other members of the team to contribute to the decision-making process. This not only increases job satisfaction by involving employees or team members in what's going on, but it also helps to develop people's skills. Employees and team members feel in control of their own destiny, such as the promotion they desire, and so are motivated to work hard by more than just a financial reward.

As participation takes time, this approach can take more time, but often the end result is better. The approach can be most suitable where team working is essential, and quality is more important than speed to market or productivity.

Lewin's study found that participative leadership, also known as democratic leadership, is generally the most effective leadership style. Democratic leaders offer guidance to group members, but they also participate in the group and allow input from other group members. In Lewin's study, children in this group were less productive than the members of the authoritarian group, but their contributions were of a much higher quality.

Participative leaders encourage group members to participate, but retain the final say over the decision-making process. Group members feel engaged in the process and are more motivated and creative.

5. Laissez-Faire (Delegative) Leadership.

This French phrase means "leave it be" and is used to describe a leader who leaves his or her colleagues to get on with their work. It can be effective if the leader monitors what is being achieved and communicates this back to his or her team regularly. Most often, laissez-faire leadership works for teams in which the individuals are very experienced and skilled self-starters. Unfortunately, it can also refer to situations where managers are not exerting sufficient control.

Delegative leaders offer little or no guidance to group members and leave decision-making up to group members. While this style can be effective in situations where group members are highly qualified in an area of expertise, it often leads to poorly defined roles and a lack of motivation.

6. People/Relations-Oriented Leadership.

This style of leadership is the complete opposite of task-oriented leadership. In people-oriented leadership, the leader is totally focused on organizing, supporting and developing the people that re on the leader's team. This style utilizes a participative approach and as such, tends to lead to good teamwork and creative collaboration. In practice, most leaders use both task-oriented and people-oriented styles of leadership.

7. Servant Leadership.

This term, coined by Robert Greenleaf in the 1970s, describes a leader who is often not formally recognized as such. When someone, at any level within an organization, leads simply by virtue of meeting the needs of his or her team, he or she is described as a "servant leader". In many ways, servant leadership is a form of democratic leadership, as the whole team tends to be involved in decision-making.

Supporters of the servant leadership model suggest it is an important way ahead in a world where values are increasingly important, in which servant leaders achieve power on the basis of their values and ideals. Others believe that in competitive leadership situations, people practicing servant leadership will often find themselves left behind by leaders using other leadership styles.

8. Task-Oriented Leadership.

A highly task-oriented leader focuses only on getting the job done, and can be quite autocratic. He or she will actively define the work and the roles required, put structures in place, plan, organize and monitor. However, as task-oriented leaders spare little thought for the well-being of their teams, this approach can suffer many of the flaws of autocratic leadership, with difficulties in motivating and retaining staff.

9. Transactional Leadership.

This style of leadership starts with the idea that team members agree to obey their leader totally, when they take on a job: the "transaction" is (usually) that the organization pays the team members in return for their effort and compliance. You have a right to "punish" the team members if their work doesn't meet the pre-determined standard.

Team members can do little to improve their job satisfaction under transactional leadership. The leader could give team members some control of their income/reward by using incentives that encourage even higher standards or greater productivity. Alternatively, a transactional leader could practice "management by exception", whereby, rather than rewarding better work, he or she would take corrective action if the required standards were not met.

Transactional leadership is really just a way of managing rather a true leadership style as the focus is on short-term tasks. It has serious limitations for knowledge-based or creative work, but remains a common style in many organizations.

10. Transformational Leadership.

A person with this leadership style is a true leader who inspires his or her team constantly with a shared vision of the future. Transformational leaders are highly visible, and spend a lot of time communicating. They do not necessarily lead from the front, as they tend to delegate responsibility amongst their team. While their enthusiasm is often infectious, they generally need to be supported by "details people".

In many organizations, both transactional and transformational leadership are needed. The transactional leaders (or managers) ensure that routine work is done reliably, while the transformational leaders look after initiatives that add value.

11. Ethical/4P Leadership.

In this leadership style, the character or personality of a good ethical organization (or leader) is defined. The leader (or organization) has a clearly defined purpose, has at its core a desire not to harm or treat the planet as a sacred resource, places great importance on its people and focuses on probity or the act of doing well. One example of an ethical leader would be Anita Roddick, the founder of The Body Shop.[119]

So, What Type of a Leader Are You?

Where does your leadership style lie? Do you tend to be more autocratic or democratic? Do you tend to be transactional or transformational? Don't make

---

[119] www.businessballs.com/ethical_management_leadership.htm.

the mistake of relying on the style you BELIEVE you are. Confirm your belief by asking people close to you then you must adjust your style to the type of leader that you believe will be the most productive for you. Here's a strong hint --- the ideal style falls in the bottom right quadrant of the graph below.

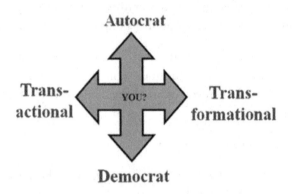

Grandma Would Transform your Business in ONE Day

Following is a blog that I wrote back in 2015 that was one of my most well-received. I wanted to share this, for all you entrepreneurs and small business owners who are reading this book. Enjoy!

I have been thinking (and writing) a lot lately about ways that entrepreneurs, start-ups, business owners, and leaders can improve their business (go from good to great) by practicing exceptional business leadership skills.

To transform your business, now is the perfect time to go back to your start-up roots and rekindle the passion you had when you first launched your business.

Go "old school" to revisit the time-tested to grow a successful business that you may have gotten away from in the hustle and bustle of operating your business.

You can't get any more "old school" then asking: **"What would grandma do to transform my business, if I put her in charge for just one day?** So, let's explore what would happen if we put grandma in charge of your business (team) for JUST ONE DAY...

Embrace the Art of Gift Giving

Grandma would come to the office bearing gifts. Did you ever bake and bring in a homemade apple pie (yum, pie!) for your employees? Did you ever knit a sweater to celebrate an employee's birthday, or a special accomplishment?

Grandma always knew how to welcome people in her home with open arms. She made us feel special, wanted, and appreciated! How do YOU make your employees, clients, vendors, and partners all feel special?

Roll Out the Welcome Mat

Do you make your newly hired employees feel good about joining your team? How (if at all) do you welcome each and every one of your new hires? I'm not talking about shaking their hand as you lead them to their cubicle (cage) but MUCH more.

Do you take new employees out for breakfast their first day on the job?? How about taking the time to walk them around and introduce them to everyone? Do you check in with them in the middle and end of their first day on the job, to see how they are doing? At the end of their very first day on the job, do you ask your new hires what their experiences were like?

Hug Your Employees

We're not talking about physically hugging. In today's politically correct business culture that would mean opening yourself up to a sexual harassment claim. Do you emotionally embrace your people, make them feel good about you as their leader?

Check out "**Hug Your People**" by Jack Mitchell, for a starting reference point.

After all, your people spend more time at your place of business then they do in their own homes. Show them how much you appreciate them. Grandma cooked us our favorite meals. You can certainly reward, recognize, coach, mentor, and promote people. Give people increased responsibilities. Make all your employees feel equally special. DON'T pull a grandma and show favoritism to that one most favored grandchild. In the grandparent business, it's called providing unconditional love. In best business practices, it's called visionary business leadership.

Love Your Family (People) Unconditionally

Your people are going to make mistakes. Instead of punishing them, follow grandma's lead. Encourage them to be their best, take risks, embrace the discomfort of tackling the unknown. Challenge them to fail "GREATLY!" by implementing "STRETCH" goals in your people's performance management planning and goal-setting.

Grandma would go even farther. She would get to know their hopes and fears, talk to them often about the very real challenges they face in balancing their home and work life. Lend a shoulder to lean on, and provide an ear to bend as you truly **LISTEN.**

Sit Up Straight, Make Eye Contact and Behave

Grandma would provide much-needed executive coaching and professional development best practices to your management team. She would start by telling you to stop slouching, sit up straight and make eye contact! Be proud of who you are and your accomplishments "dearie" and always look others square in the eyes so they can trust you.

Grandma would remind you that your word is a promise, and trust is absolutely critical not only in business, but in life. She would then lecture you (lovingly) about how we could all do with a bit more trust in one another these days. She'd also add that it's important to say "please" and "thank you."

She would remind us the business world would not have had to deal with Bernie Madoff, Enron, Adelphia, Global Crossing, Halliburton, British Petroleum, etc. if more of us business owners acted with the highest ethical standards.

She would pinch your cheek and suggest that the most profitable businesses operate in the highest ethical standards and true leaders take their business along a course guided with a strong moral compass you summarized as "DO GOOD."

No Pink Slips...Just Pink Booties

Grandmas don't fire, layoff, right-size, down-size, re-engineer, off-shore, or outsource their people...ever! Once they bring you into the family, you are family. If an employee was valuable enough to bring into your organization, then they should always be able to contribute especially if you develop them professionally. Every grandma knows that! They don't believe in pink slips, but they may just knit your infant a pair of pink booties.

Understand the Value of a Dollar

Grandma survived the Great Depression. Could you?

Manage your business finances with a militant view towards keeping your debt down. Watch your cash flow and manage your business expenses. Take advantage of limited time free offers, make purchases using bonus points, take advantage of promotional offers, and use coupons. Have you ever heard the phrase: "Watch your pennies and the dollars will take care of themselves?" That's a grandmother speaker. They also like to say: "penny wise, pound foolish." That means NOT cutting back on the expenses needed to take care of your people. In fact, a grandma would know it makes brilliant business sense to spend money for special gifts on your employees to make them feel special and appreciated.

Conflict Resolution with Fresh-Baked Cookies

If two co-workers aren't getting along, Grandma would make them sit together and work through their issues over her freshly baked cookies and homemade hot cocoa. Honestly, how could ANYONE stay angry after enjoying piping hot chocolate chip cookies served with steamy homemade hot cocoa (and whipped cream?)

Well, the workday is winding down and Grandma's work is done. Your people are happier than ever, your customers feel a lot better about you and your business, and things are humming along. Grandma would love to stay, but she has to get home to watch **Wheel of Fortune** and Skype with her grandson, who just left for his first year of college.

She's turning your business back over to you, and asks when you are coming to visit. You tell her "soon grandma." First, you have to plan employee appreciation luncheon, schedule a client roadshow, plan a summer town hall meeting, and find worthwhile causes for you and your employees to get active in.

Watching her treat people the way she does all day long really affected you. You promise her you'll change as a business owner. She just smiles, pats you on the cheek and says: "of course you will." Because that's what grandmas do.

Resources on Effective Leadership

- www.leadershipnow.com
- http://leadershipskillcenter.com
- www.leadingtoday.org
- www.hbs.edu/leadership/database
- www.emergingleader.com
- www.leader-values.com
- www.franklincoveycoaching.com/4_roles_of_leadership

A Final Thought...

"If I have seen further, it is by standing on the shoulders of giants." - *Sir Isaac Newton*

19. World-Class Culture

Want to build a culture based on being compassionate and a workplace people will want to work at. Begin by listing all of the qualities that you want your organization to be known for, aspire to become. These desirable characteristics are your organization's "**brand attributes,**" your Unique Value Proposition.

Define the type of people you want to work with as suppliers, contractors, vendors, the media...everyone! Describe who your ideal employee is. Create an organizational "ideal employee profile." Next, identify which type of clients do you want to serve?

Your Vision Statement

Your organization's vision statement is used to explain what you want to be/become. It is entirely aspirational. Your Vision should inspire the hearts of those people who work for you, and engage with you/your business.

Example: Norfolk Southern: "Be the safest, most customer-focused and most successful transportation company in the world."

Your Mission Statement

Defines what your organization does and does not do, and who you do it for.

(Example. The U.S. Tennis Association: "Promote and develop the growth of tennis."

Mission statements drive everything your organization does. They should be simple, direct, and operative.

Other Really Great Examples:

PATAGONIA

"Build the best product, cause no unnecessary harm, use business to inspire and implement solutions to the environmental crisis." WHY do they believe this? To quote the company: "A love of wild and beautiful places (what their business model is based on) demands participation in the fight to save them."

WARBY PARKER

"Was founded with a rebellious spirit and a lofty objective to offer designer eyewear at a revolutionary price, while leading the way for socially-conscious business."

INVISIONAPP.com

Their CORE VALIUES are so important to them they post them up-front on the home page of their website.

HONEST TEA

"HT seeks to create and promote great tasting healthier organic beverages. We strive to grow our business with the same honesty and integrity we use to craft our products, with sustainability and great taste for all."

LG – LIFE IS GOOD

"Spread the power of optimism." They put their money where their mouth is, by donating 10% of the Company's net profits to kids in need. Their organizational values are so important to their culture, the place their values in their company name.

IKEA

"Make everyday life better" for their customers.

NORDSTROM

"Nordstrom works relentlessly to give customers the most compelling shopping experience possible."

Creating a Great Culture

List all of the qualities that you want your ideal employees to have. Then define the types of people that you want to work with (and don't) in terms of suppliers, contractors, vendors, the media, and service providers.

Once you define your organizational culture, you MUST communicate it by stating your organizational values everywhere, from your job descriptions, to your website, employee orientation handbook, as well as your social media, press releases, and website.

The Power in Storytelling

One of the most powerful tools at your organization's disposal to create a compassionate organization is to use the art of STORYTELLING to explain your values, ethics, history, and all the things that make you unique, invaluable, and memorable.

Begin by chronicling your organization's history. Key dates, how it was formed, its founders, their passions, values, ethics. As you do so, be sure to list your organization's defining symbols, icons, deeper meanings, founder's values and beliefs. Identify the key milestones and achievements throughout your organizational life. How does your organization give back to/engage your local communities, causes you support, employee volunteer work?

20. Is Your Organization Compassionate? Take a Quiz

Does your organization foster compassion or callousness? Find out by taking this quiz which measures the level of compassion in an organization. It is based on more than 10 years of research on compassion and organizations by the research collaborative **CompassionLab** and the **Center for Positive Organizational Scholarship** at the University of Michigan Ross School of Business.

Complete the quiz online at http://greatergood.berkeley.edu/quizzes/take_quiz/11 and submit your answers for an assessment.

21. Build a World Class Culture

It seems as if "*__culture-building__*" is all the rave in organizations these days.

Not sure why it's taken so long for organizations to re-consider the cultures they created. This is something anyone tasked with running a business, leading a team, or recruiting and retaining top talent deals with on a nearly constant basis...or SHOULD.

In my prior life in Corporate America I led many teams through significant transformation, and in my work as an organizational coach I have talked to thousands of business owners, partners, executives, leaders, and HR folks about their challenges building a place that rising stars would want to work at.

They are looking for a new breed of worker. They want (NEED, in fact) people who WANT to commit to them unconditionally, but won't because of their flawed cultures.

They're looking to recruit (and keep) people who exhibit exceptional characteristics including: strive to perform at the height of their abilities, share their employer's ethics and values, are willing to take risks and embrace challenges, want to contribute to their organization's risk, perform meaningful work, and care enough about that organization to do everything in their power for the organization to succeed.

But a major challenge organizations face that often prevents them from being able to recruit Superhero employees is an abject lack of empathy and caring. These organizations don't respect their employees, they don't invest in them with training and development, don't offer coaching/mentoring programs, don't believe in job rotations, offer little in the way of meaningful benefits, don't believe in self-directed/managed teams, don't strive to build trust, don't subscribe to ethical behavior, nor do they have a moral compass (other than maximizing profits and reducing costs.)

Making matters even more complicated when it pertains to building a strong culture is, there are actually two types of culture. The formal culture is entirely aspirational. It's what the organization WANTS to be/become, or believes it is. That may have little or no basis in reality, when factoring considering its informal culture. The informal culture is how the organization feel like, and how it behaves when it thinks no one is watching.

Is it any wonder therefore that talented employees would not be caught dead committing to employers that only have to offer stifling, toxic, dead end cultures with no motivation, challenging work, shared sense of mission, teamwork and collaboration, advancement, causes they care passionately about?

Does this describe YOU...your employees...where you work?

If so, here's why...according to a 2015 survey by the **Human Capital Media Advisory Group**:

- Only 44% of HR practitioners admitted their organizations hire people who "fit" their culture.
- Even though 70% of the survey's respondents said their organizations wanted to build culture, missions and values *only about a third said that culture was built into the work* their employees perform.
- Many companies (68%) said they seek to change their culture, in order to improve their employee engagement.

THAT is why I created a webinar: "Build Your World-Class Culture...NOW!"

To help you (and your organization) change your culture. Create a workplace where your people are engaged, collaborate willingly, don't harbor resentment or have political agendas, and are striving constantly to achieve maximum productivity.

Want to maximize your profits by driving revenue sky high while finding new creative ways to reduce costs?

Steps to build a world-class culture right now in your organization:

- Re-position your organization in the hearts and minds of others by revisiting your vision, mission, values.

- Define the type of people you want to work with, including suppliers, contractors, vendors, the media...everyone!
- Master your storytelling -tell what sets your organization apart. Engage others with your history, key achievements and most importantly...WHY you do what you do...**your purpose**!
- Treat your employees like *valued partners* for optimal engagement and retention.
- Implement Reward & Recognition, Coaching/Mentoring, Employee Idea, and Town Hall programs.
- Intrinsic vs Extrinsic motivation.
- Define and RECRUIT the attributes of STAR performers.

22. About Ethan

I teach individuals how to transform from good to GREAT, by helping them reach their full potential.

Here's Why:

After spending 20+ years in Corporate America in marketing and product management roles, I had a life-changing vision. I decided to pursue my passion for helping others by applying my branding, marketing, and communications expertise with my knowledge of optimizing peak performance and an almost pathological hatred for organizational dysfunction and lack of caring.

So, I formed my motivational speaking, executive coaching, business consulting and employee training and authored my first book: "**Bulletproof Your Career in Turbulent Times**."

As the Founder and President of **The Chazin Group LLC**, I am blessed to be able to give motivational talks, deliver training and professional development programs, provide one-on-one and group-based executive coaching, strategic consulting, HR, staffing, and recruiting guidance to benefit start-ups, established firms, non-profits, and NGOs.

I apply my experience leading teams through significant transformation across many industries by leveraging employee engagement for competitive success. I do this by leveraging expertise in organizational behavior, strategic planning, new business development, client relationship building, employee engagement, and emotional intelligence having served nearly all of the Fortune 500 as clients.

As an executive recruiter and career coach, I am proud to claim that I helped 12,000 job seekers find employment. I taught courses on business, organizational behavior, leadership, entrepreneurship, marketing, branding, social media, internet marketing, and business communications as a professor at NYU Polytechnic, Stevens Institute of Technology, St. Peter's University, Fordham University, Baruch College, Hunter College, and St. John's

University. Further, I gave career exploration/job search talks at 50 colleges and Universities.

I coach organizations to successfully transform using talent management and people-focused strategies, by teaching organizations to apply **WHY** and **WHAT IF** as their culture. Some of the organizations I have worked with include: J&J, PNC Bank, Calvin Klein, Goldman Sachs, CenturyLink, Chambers of Commerce, Rutgers University, the State University of New York, Small Business Development Centers, and the NYC Small Business Services.

I have entertained, informed, and challenged many professional organizations by giving talks and conducting training at: the National Assn of Women Business Owners, NJ & NY State CPA Societies, SHRM, NY Society of Security Analysts, NJ Bankers Assn to name a few.

I am a Kauffman Foundation FastTrac certified coach, and have conducted outplacement assistance programs with the Ayers Group.

I am proud to have been active in the Hoboken Rotary Club, Hoboken, Hudson County-NJ, Manhattan, and Brooklyn Chambers of Commerce, American Marketing Assn, American Management Assn and the Business Marketing Association and served on the Board of the Assn of Career Professionals of New York.

I conducted a weekly radio program entitled "**Chazin the Dream**" for start-up's and entrepreneurs, was published in numerous business publications, appeared on TV and participated in panels discussing today's contract-based workplace. I am constantly exploring industries that are experiencing job growth, and I eagerly share my often unconventional and non-traditional thoughts on the nature of work and the skills required to succeed in these transformational times.

I received my Bachelor of Arts degree in Communications from Cal. State University, East Bay and an MBA in Marketing from George Washington University.

PROFESSIONAL AFFILIATIONS & MEMBERSHIPS

- Commerce Industry Assn. of New Jersey — 2016 - Present
- Business Rainmakers MeetUp Group, *Founder* (384 members) — 2013 - 2015
- Hudson County, NJ Chamber of Commerce — 2014 - Present
- BNI: Gold Coast Chapter, Founding Member — 2013 - 2014
- Hoboken Rotary Club, Vice President — 2012 - Present
- Manhattan Chamber of Commerce, Education Committee — 2011-2012; 2016-Present
- Brooklyn Chamber of Commerce, Small Business Committee — 2009 - 2010
- Assn. of Career Professionals, NY Board Member — 2008
- Business Marketing Assn., Member — 2007 - 2008
- Cable & Telecommunications Assn. of Marketers, Member — 2007 - 2008
- American Marketing Assn., Member — 1989 - 2007
- American Management Assn., Member — 2003 - 2008

PARTNERSHIPS & CERTIFICATIONS

- Corporate Trainer, Lorman Education Services — 2016
- Corporate Trainer, Surgent — 2015-Present
- Retained Trainer, Rutgers Continuing Professional Education — 2015-Present
- Retained Trainer, Baruch Continuing Professional Studies — 2014-Present
- Certified Trainer, Marion Ewing Kauffman Organization — June, 2009

FastTrac Business Growth Venture Program

COURSES TAUGHT IN HIGHER EDUCATION

Course	Academic Institution(s)
Entrepreneurship	<ul><li>Stevens Institute of Technology</li><li>Fordham University</li><li>Coaching at business incubator of NJ City University</li></ul>
Organizational Behavior	NYU Tandon School of Engineering
Leadership	<ul><li>Fordham University</li><li>NYU</li></ul>
Social Media	Baruch College
Marketing Management	Saint Peter's University
Market Research	Saint Peter's University
Branding	Baruch College
Advertising & Sales Management	Hunter College
Internet Marketing	Baruch College
Business Communications	<ul><li>Saint John's University</li><li>Baruch College</li></ul>
Consumer Behavior	<ul><li>Baruch College</li></ul>

PROFESSIONAL TRAINING PROGRAMS

Organizations	Program Topics
• IFEL Next Level 2017 conference	Eight Strategies to Motivate Your People.
• NJ Society CPAs. Annual Conf. 2014 • NJ Society CPAs-Bergen, NJ Chpt. Fall 2015 Kick-Off event. Keynote Speaker • NJ/NY Franchise Expo 2014.	Brand New YOU: Market Yourself for Career Success.
• Society of Human Resource Mgt, Central NJ – April, 2016 • NJ Bankers Assn HR Conference – October, 2016	Diversity & Inclusion: Building a 5-Generation Culturally Blended American Workforce
• Calvin Klein Global Supply Team 2014 • J&J Corp. Real Estate & Strat. Planning 2015 • National Assn. Insurance & Financial Advisors Feb. 2015	Training: Team-building, problem-solving, communications, conflict resolution
• Saint Barnabas Medical Center • Western Area Power Authority	Team-Building
Garden State Council NJ Society of Human Resource Management	Ethical Behavior for Lasting Competitive Advantage
Jersey City Medical Center	Professionalism
Goldman Sachs – Jersey City, NJ	Market Yourself for Career Success. 2010.

Newark Community Health Center	Organizational Ethics & Values
• National Assn. of Women Business Owners-New York Chpt. • New Jersey Bankers Assn. HR Conference	Dare to be great in everything you do.
NY State Society of CPAs NextGen Conference. July, 2016.	Market Yourself for Career Success
NYU School of Professional Studies	• Branding & Marketing for Social Enterprises • World-Class Organizations • Business Ethics • Leadership for Millennial Managers • Network Like an All-Star
Kessler Rehabilitation Centers	• Emotional Intelligence • Leadership for the 21st Century
• PNC Bank • Rutgers College NJAES: Civil Engineers	Time Management
Lorman Education Services	Manage people older than you (and with more experience) Webinar. May, 2016.

Surgent McCoy - Webinars	• Market Yourself for Career Success. • Forge Powerful Relationships (Networking) • Human Capital Audit. • Innovation & Creativity. • Build a compelling marketing program.
La Casa de Don Pedro. Jersey City, NJ	The Power to Influence Others
Over 50 Colleges & Universities	• Career exploration, work readiness, and job search programs.
Queens & Brooklyn, NY Non-Profit Executives Fellowship Programs (through the Jewish Community Relations Council)	• Public Speaking • Crafting Elevator Pitches